"To the young adventurers and budding artists, May this book ignite your imagination, fill your world with color, and awaken the wonder within you. Let each stroke of your crayon be a step into the magical realm of creativity. May the pages of this book be a canvas for your dreams, and may your journey through its enchanted pages bring you joy, discovery, and endless inspiration. Happy coloring!"

Evaristo Soares

2024

This Book Belongs to:

Test Color Page

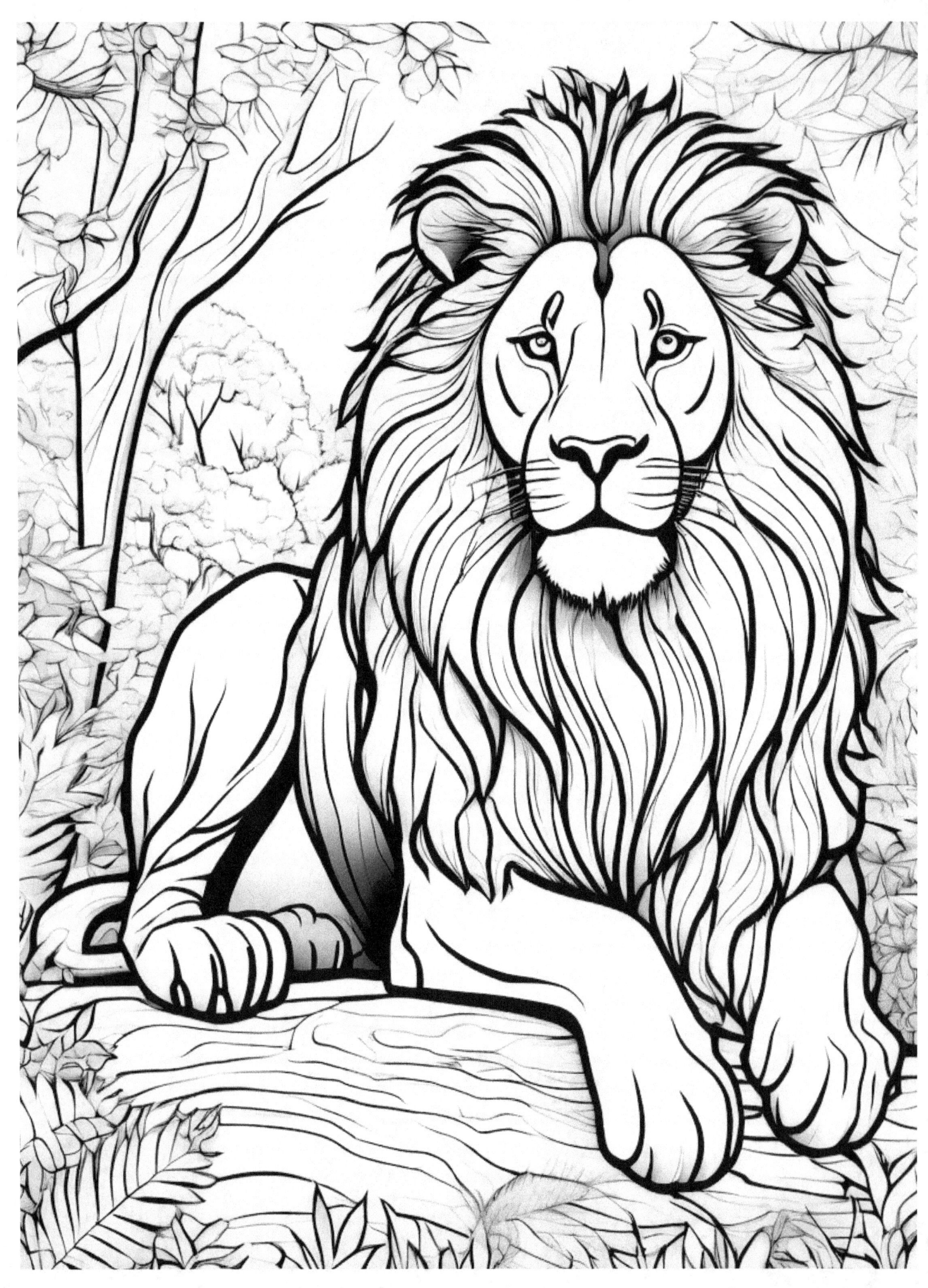

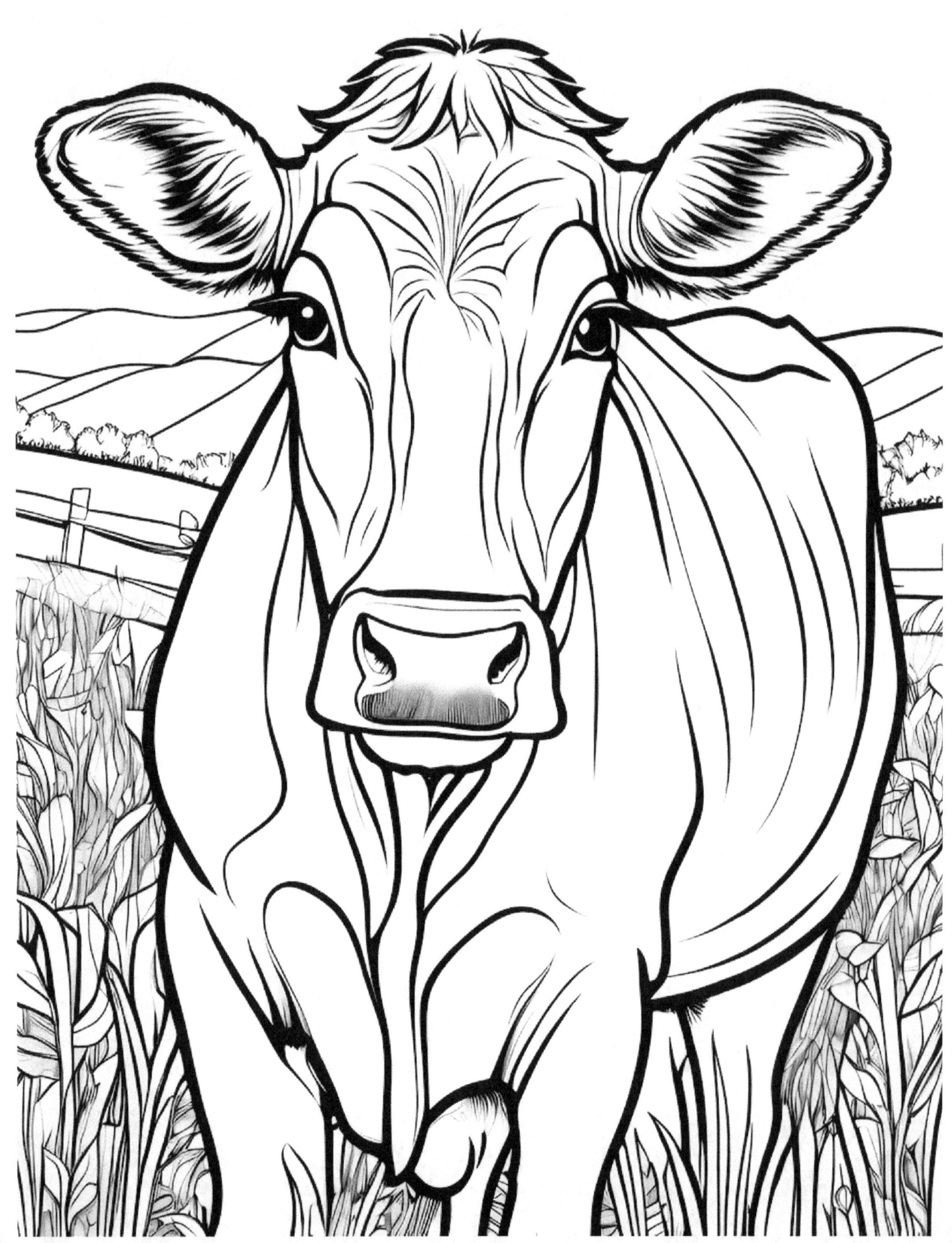

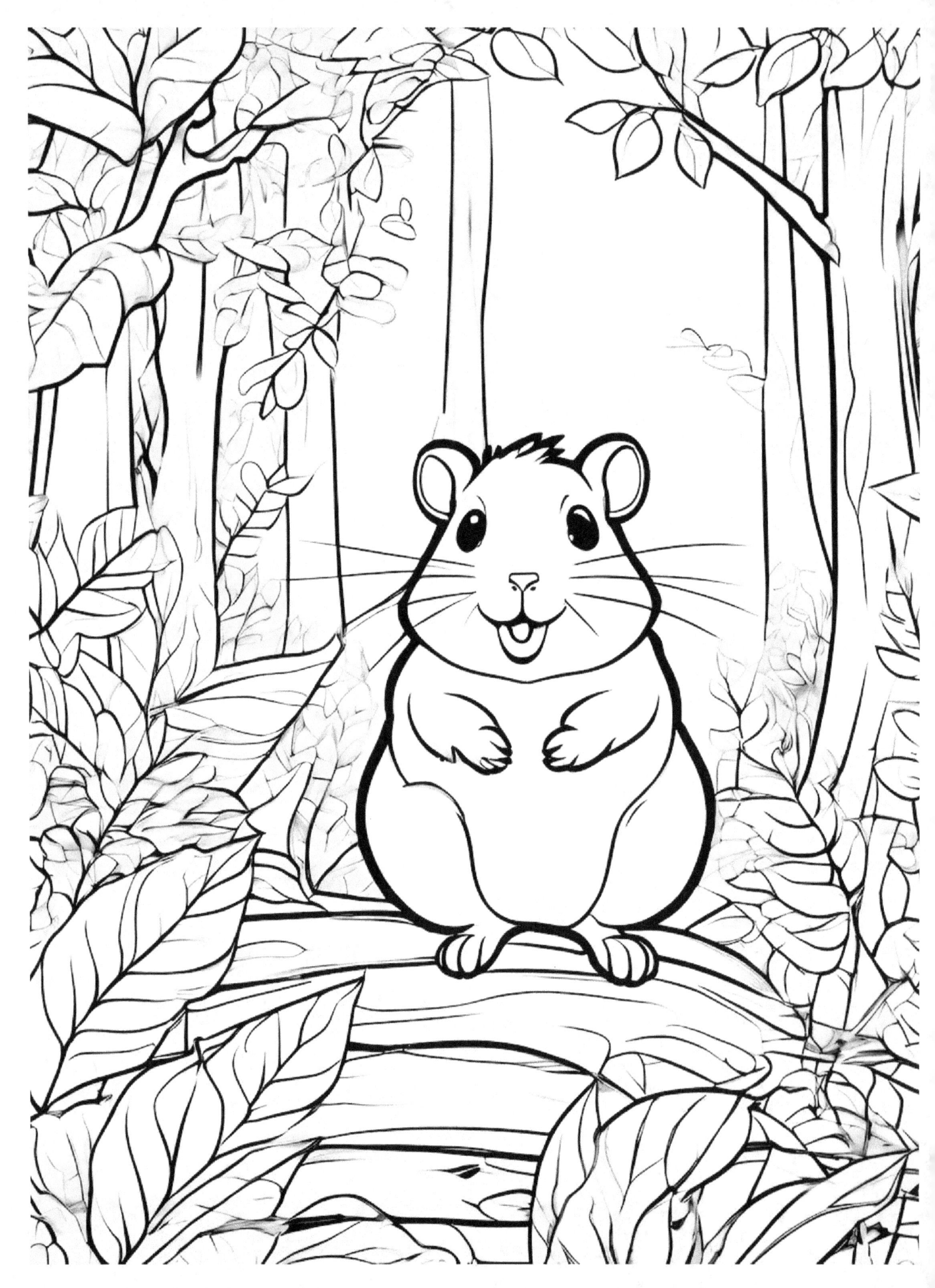

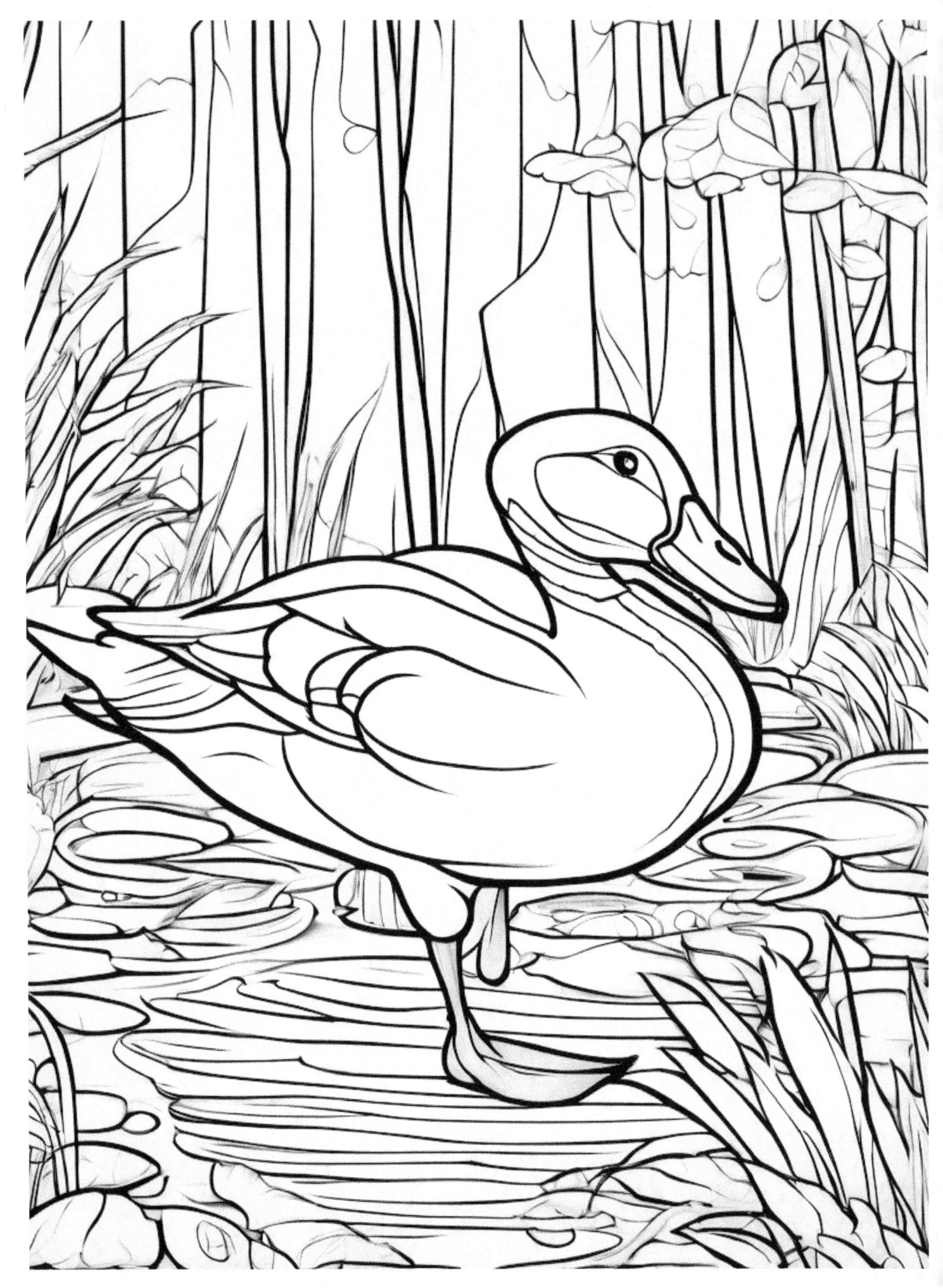

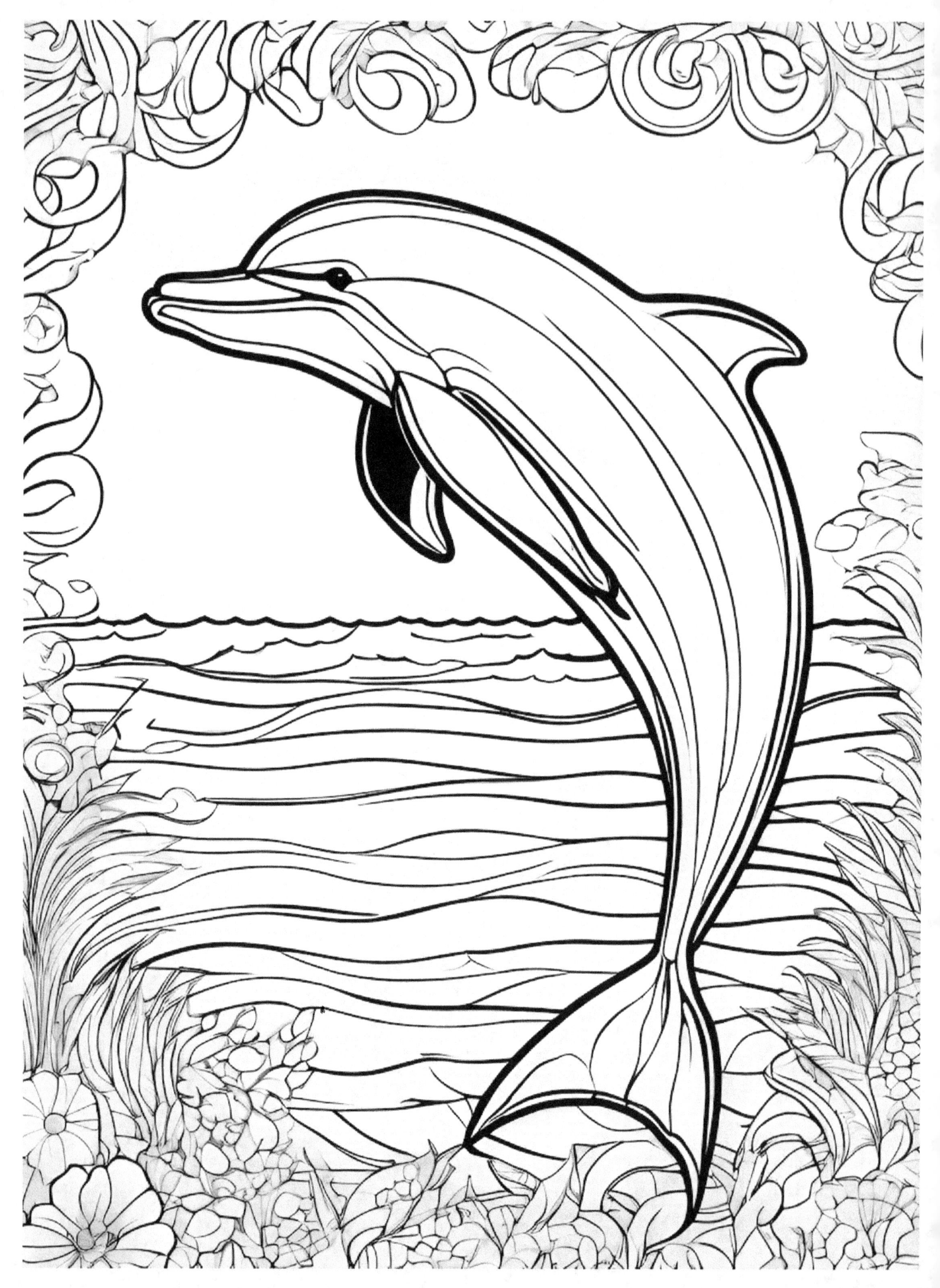

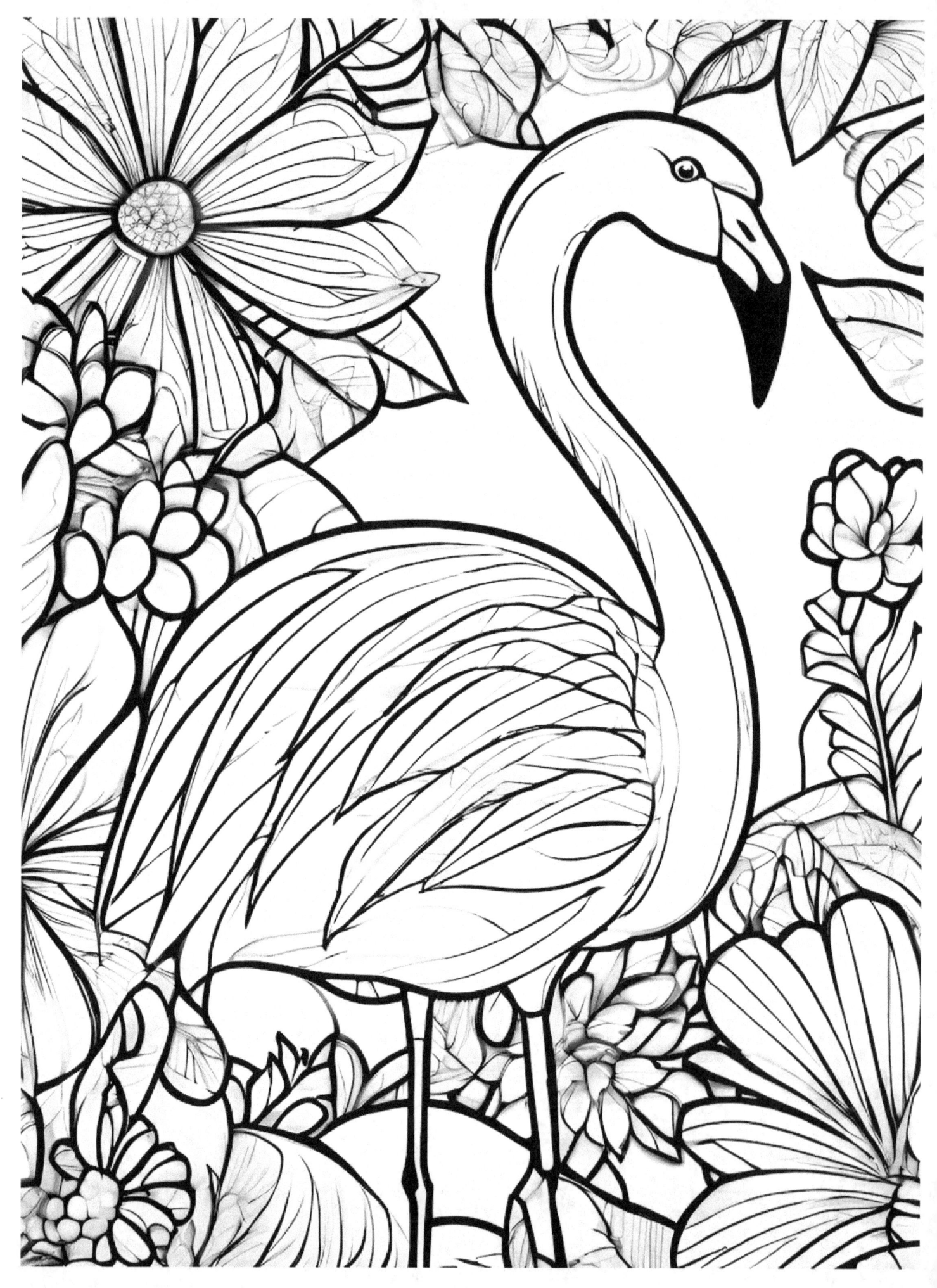

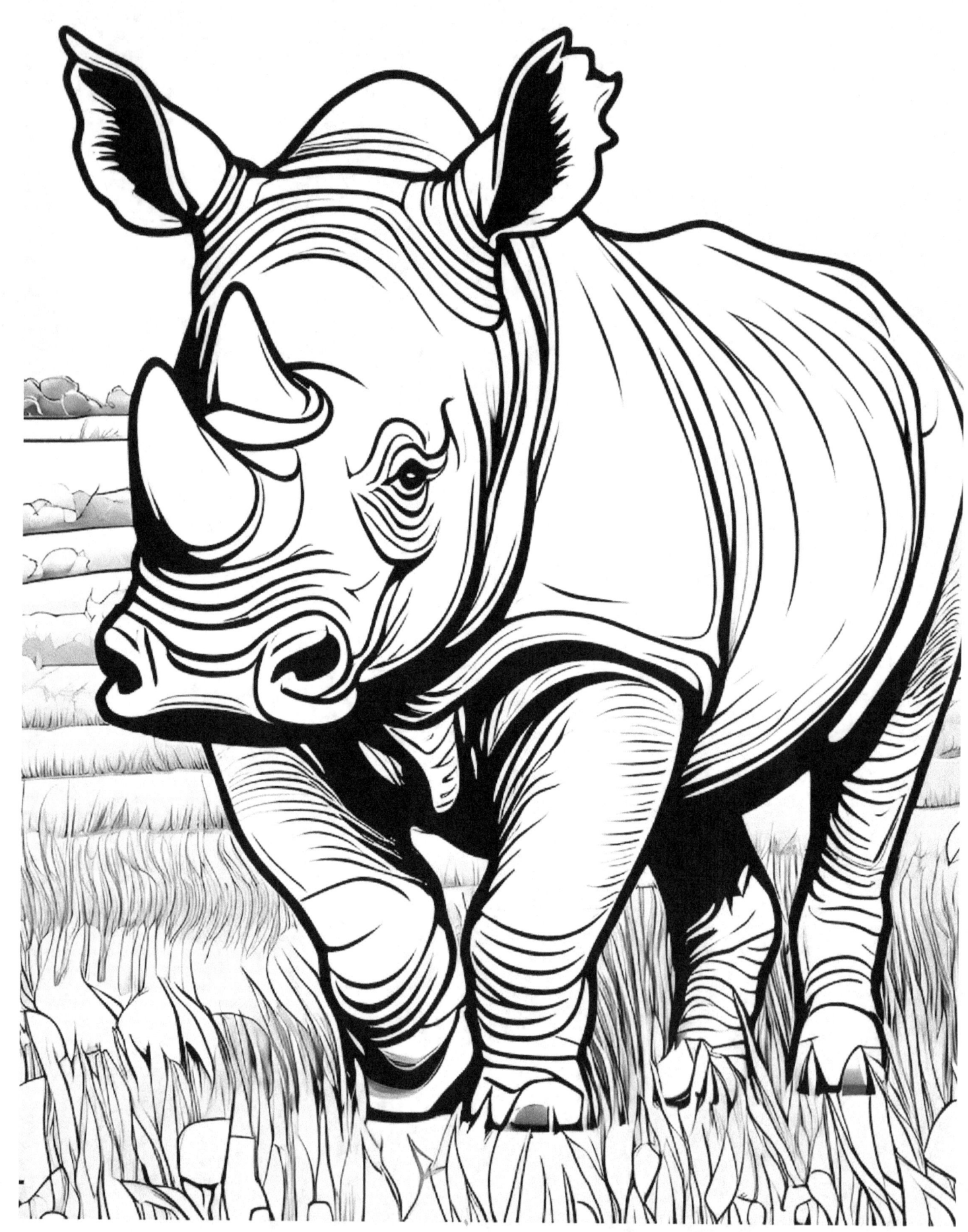

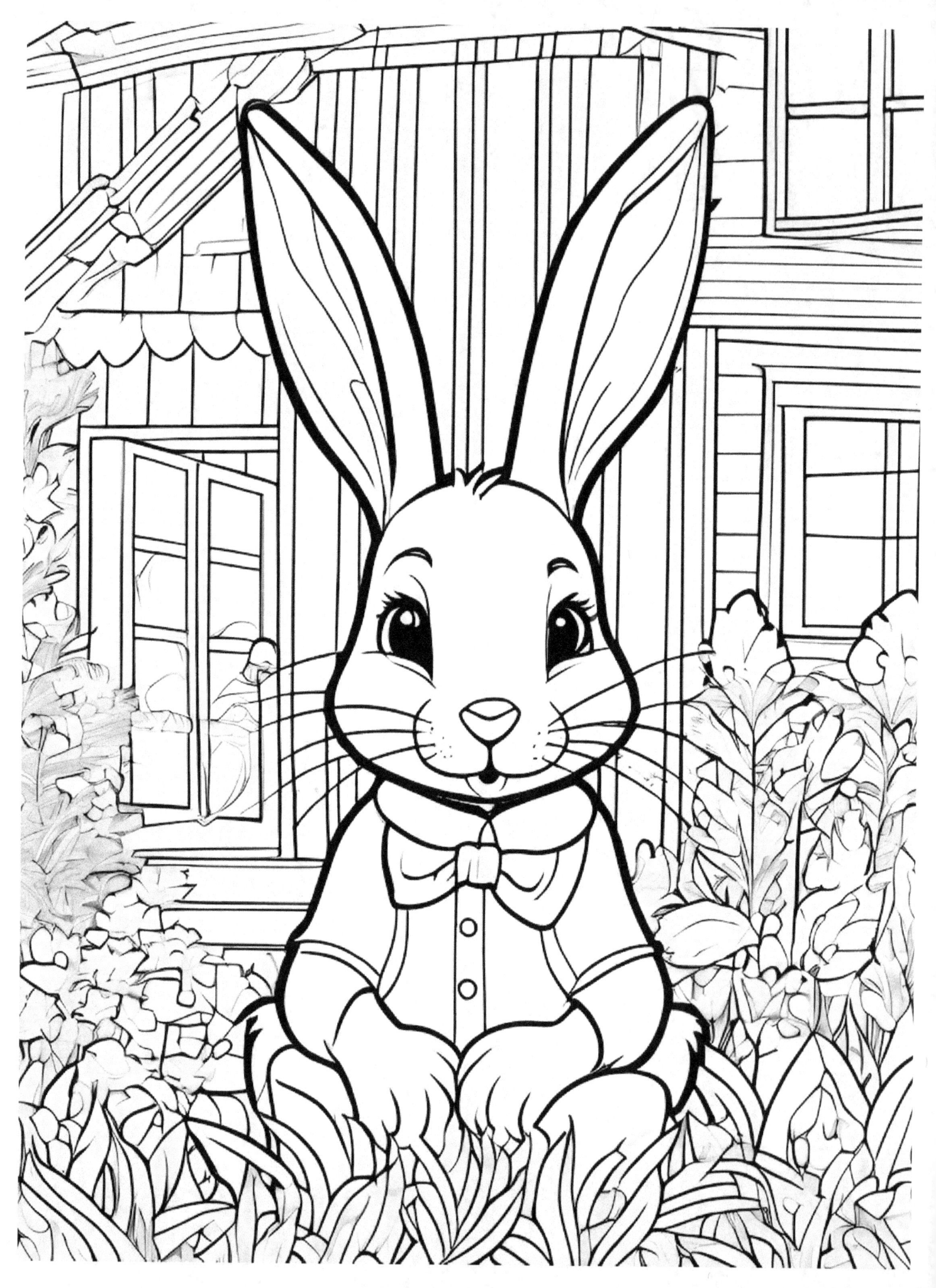

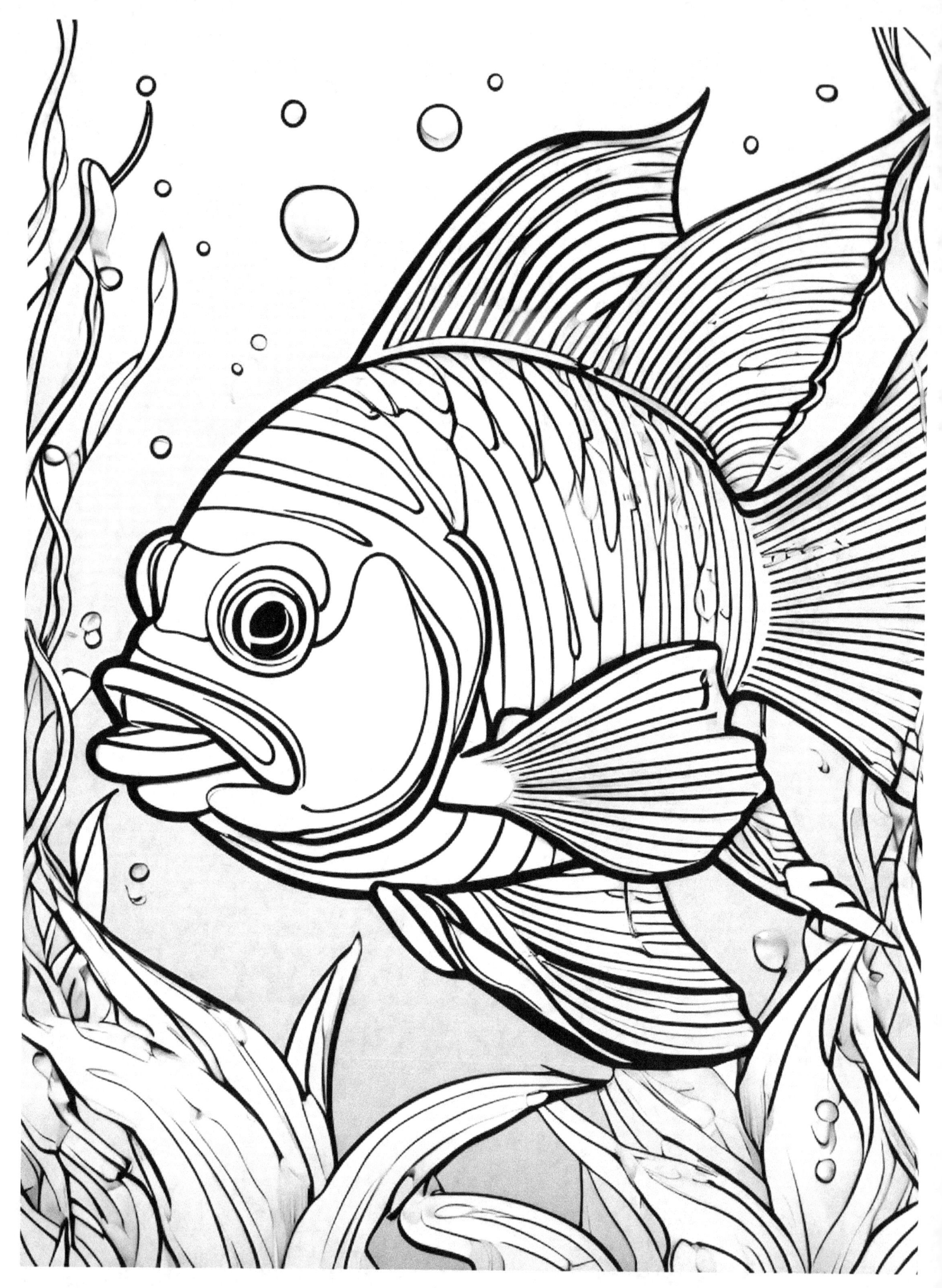

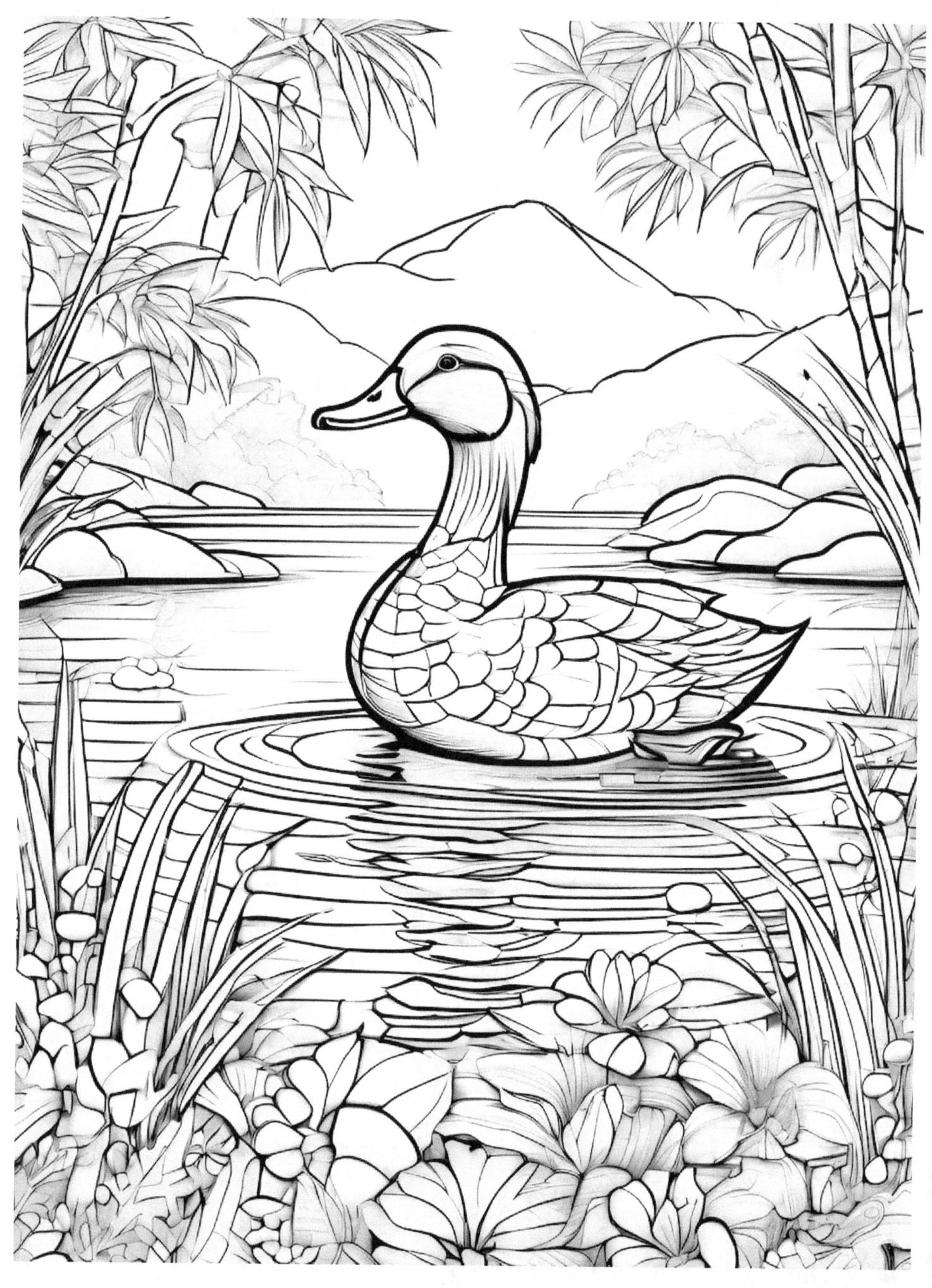

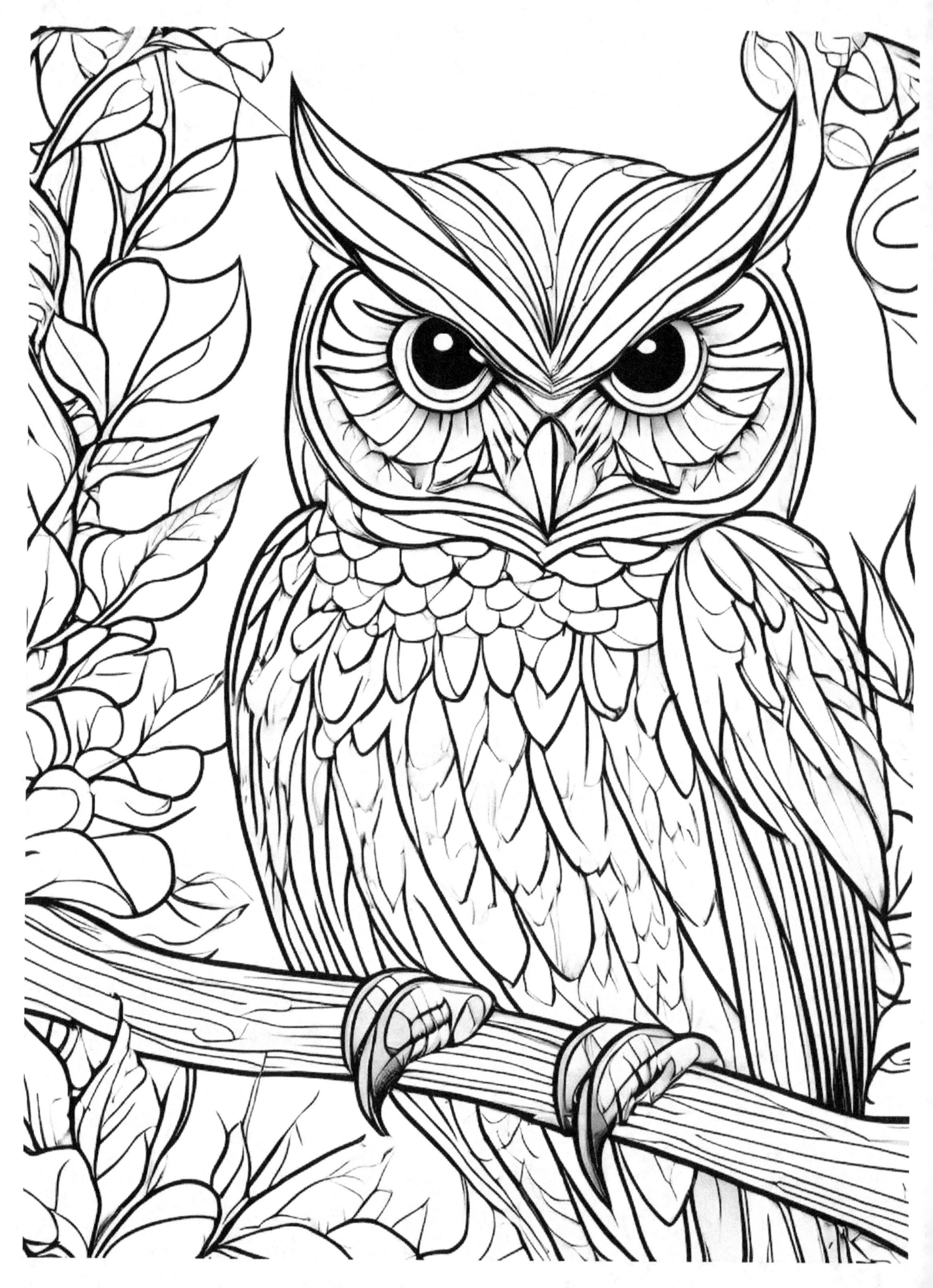

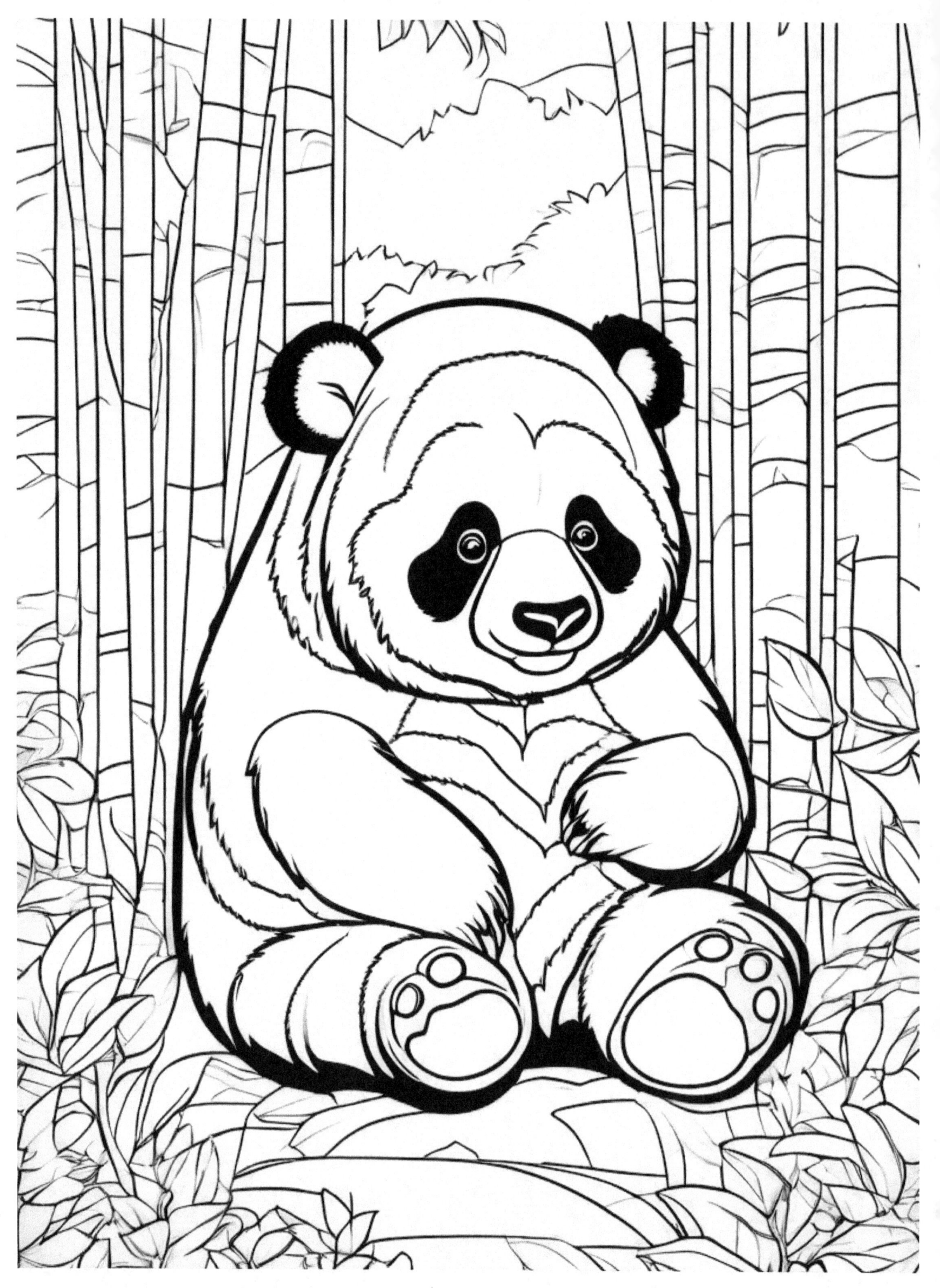

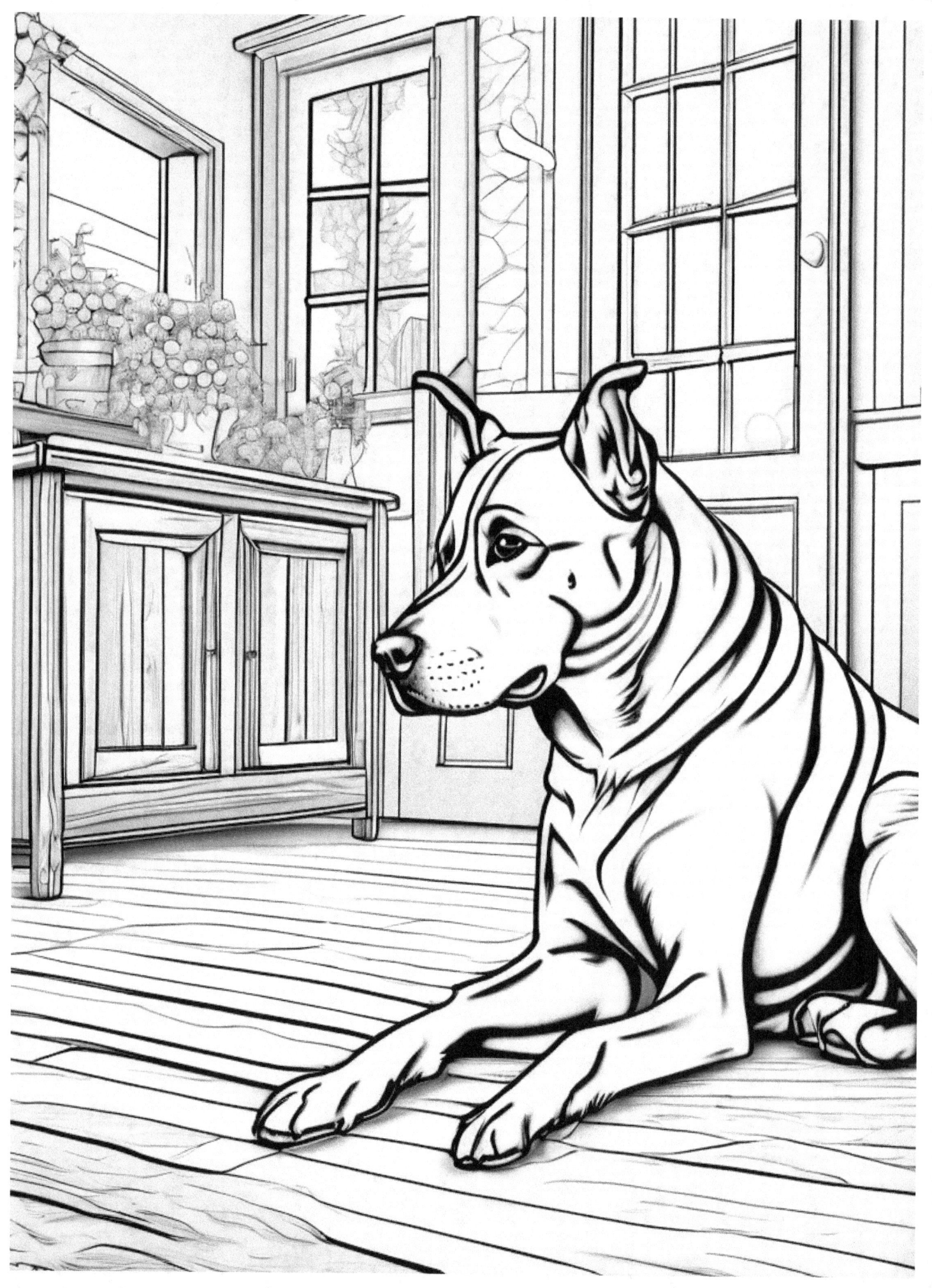

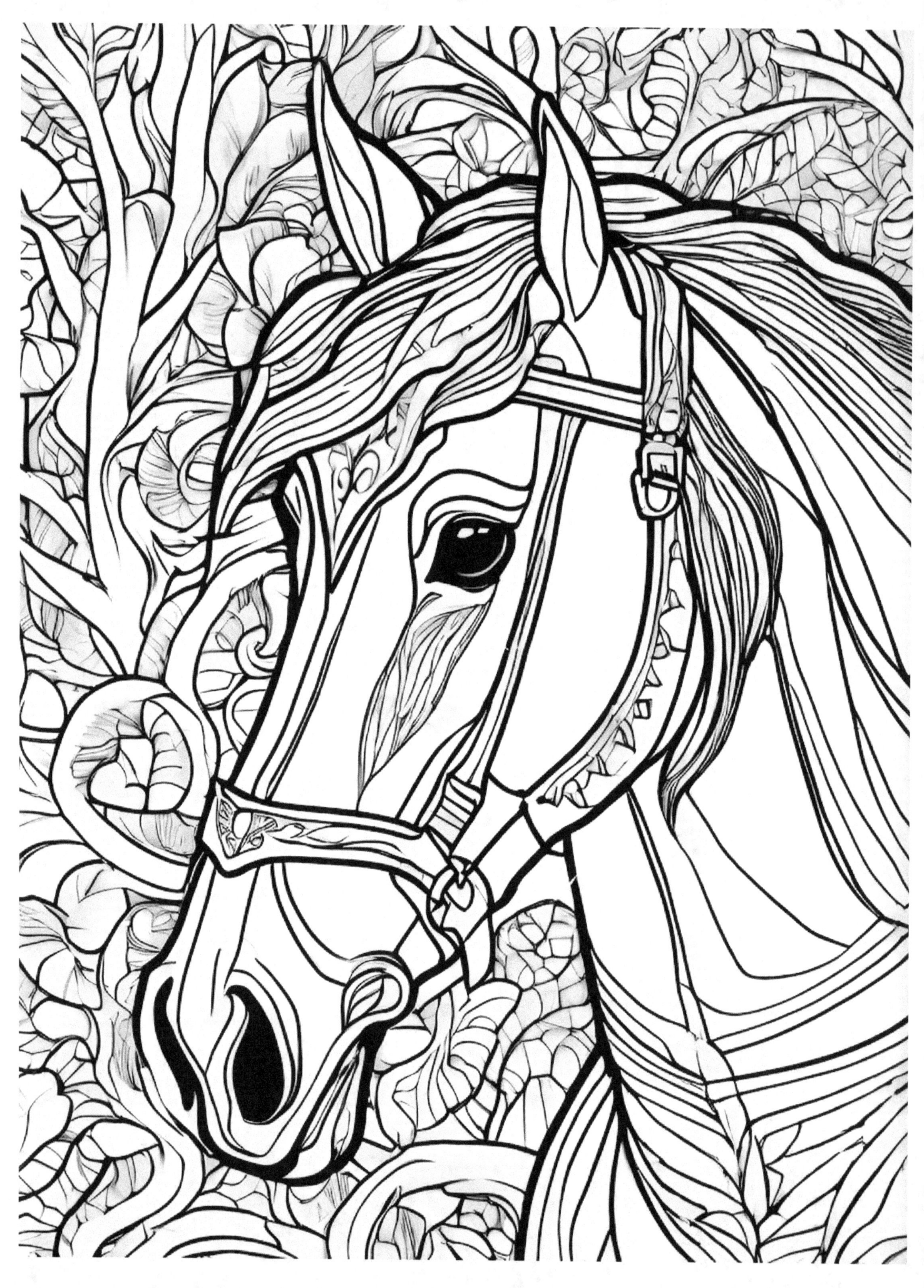

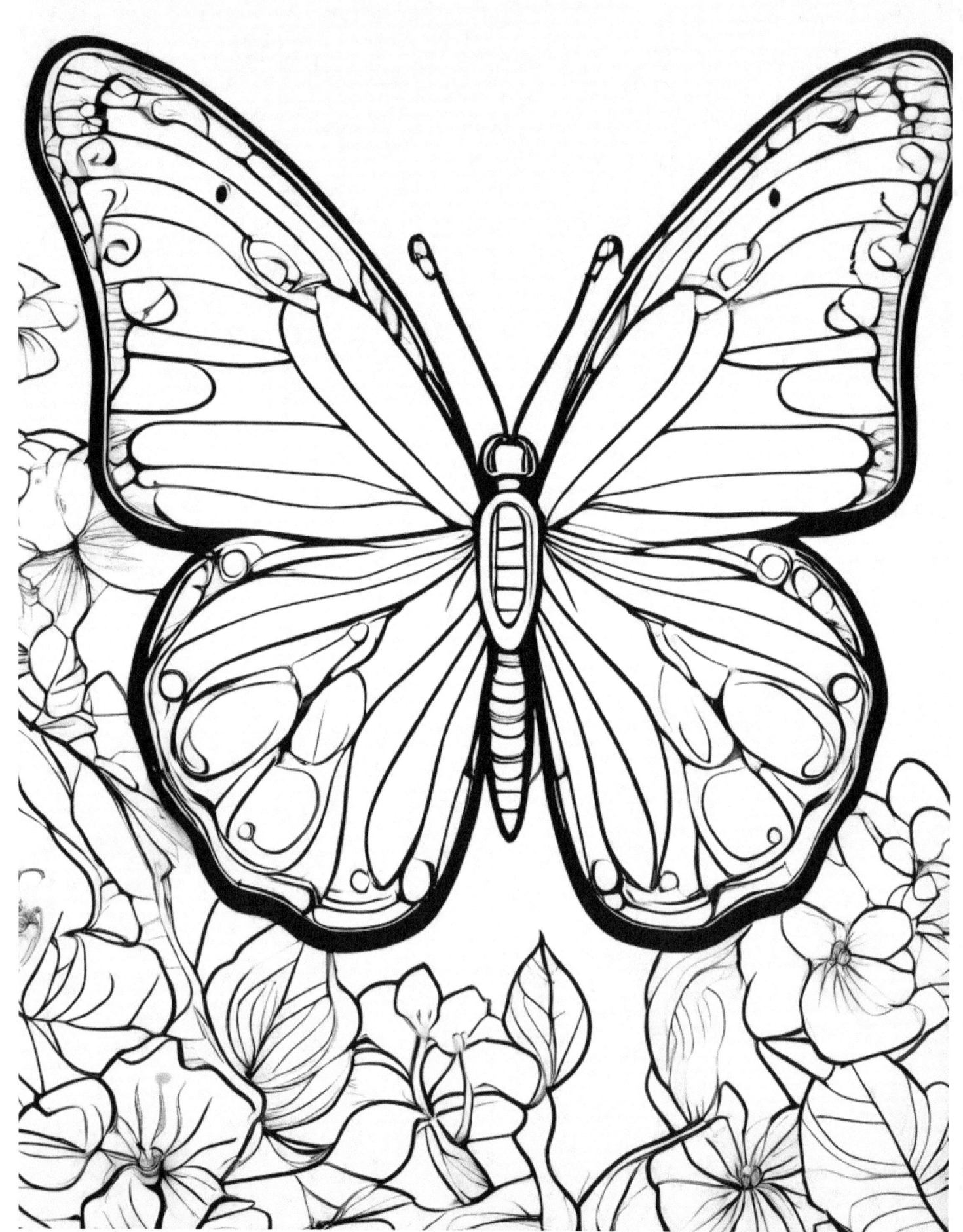

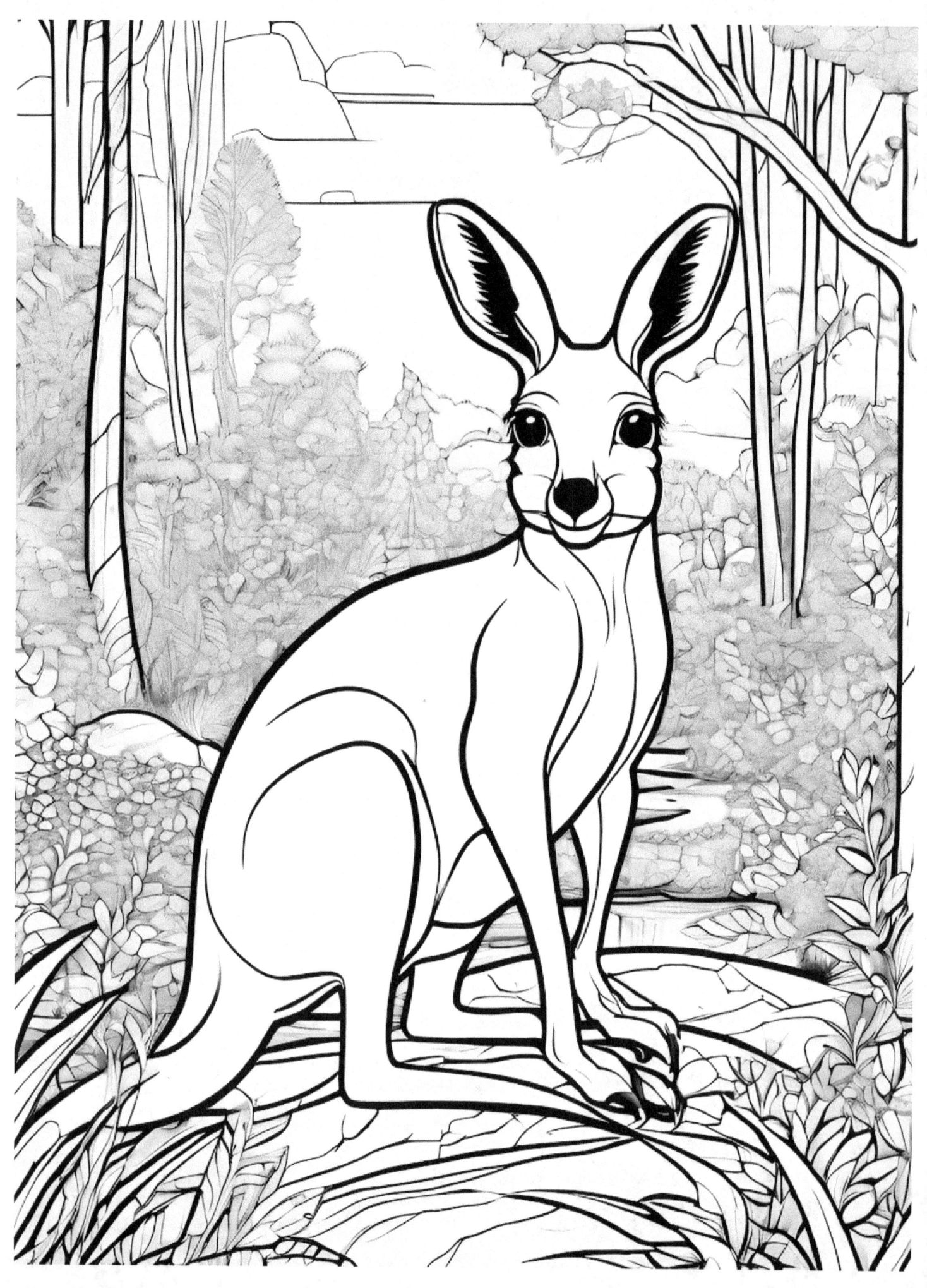

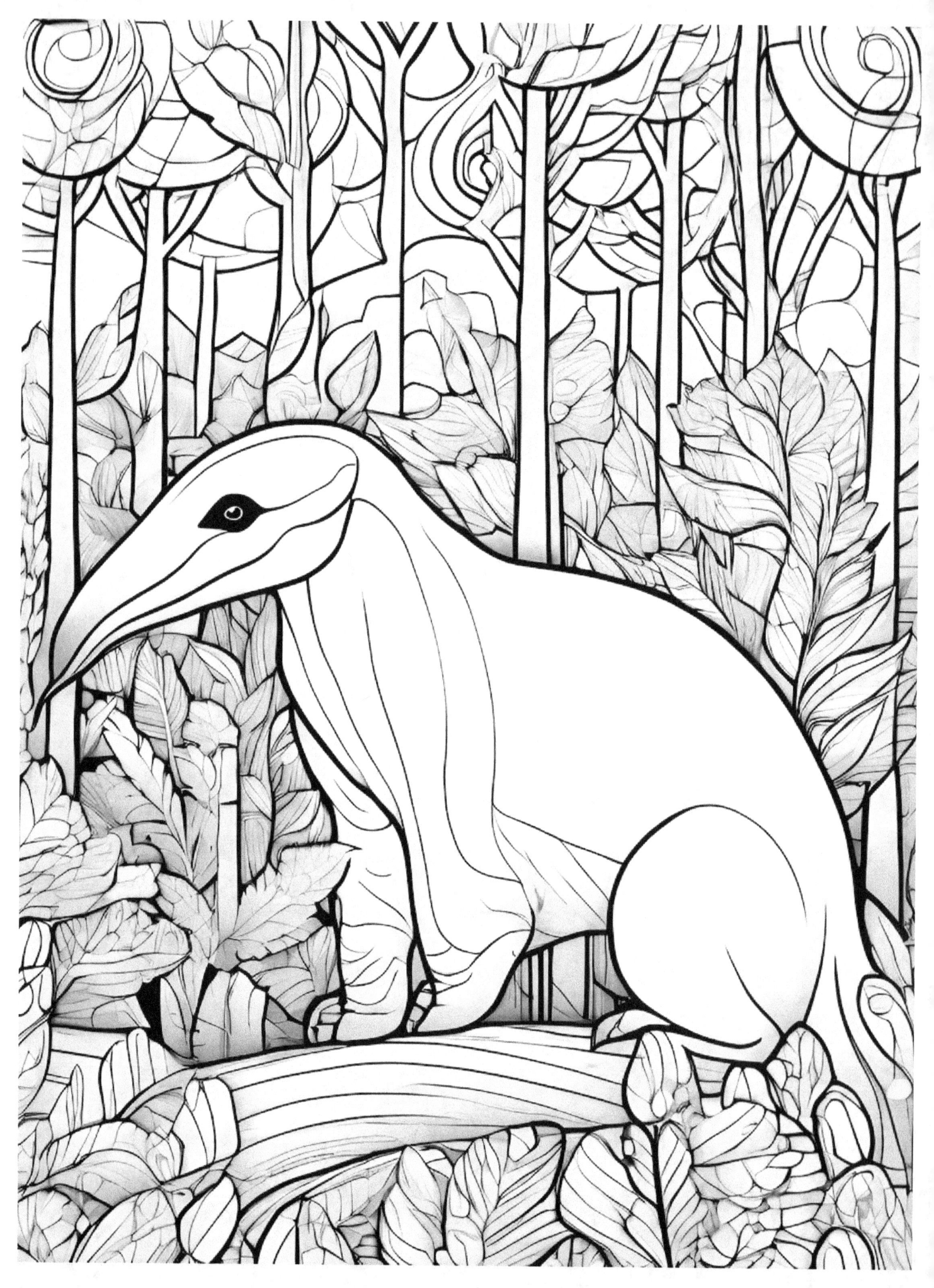

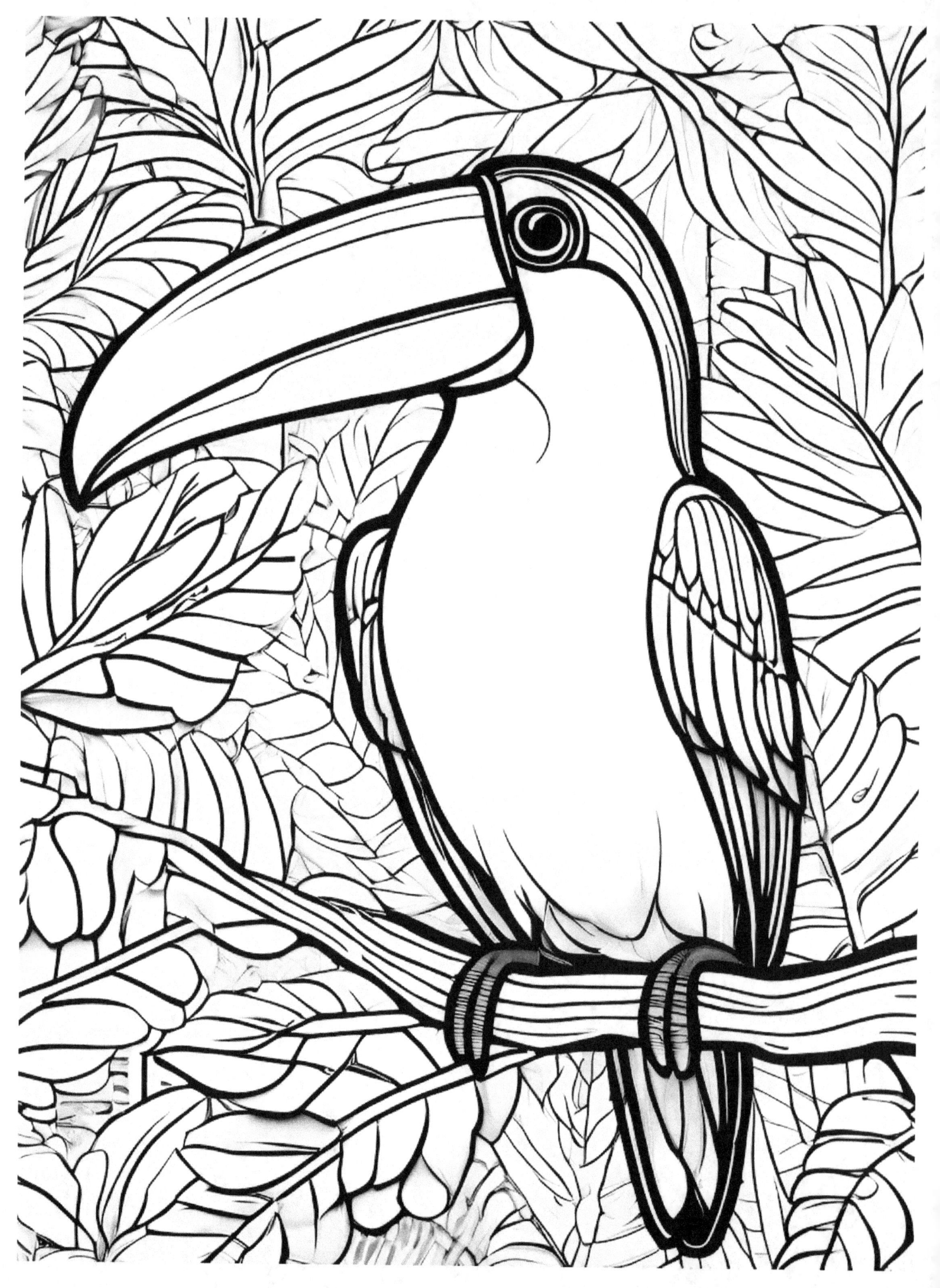

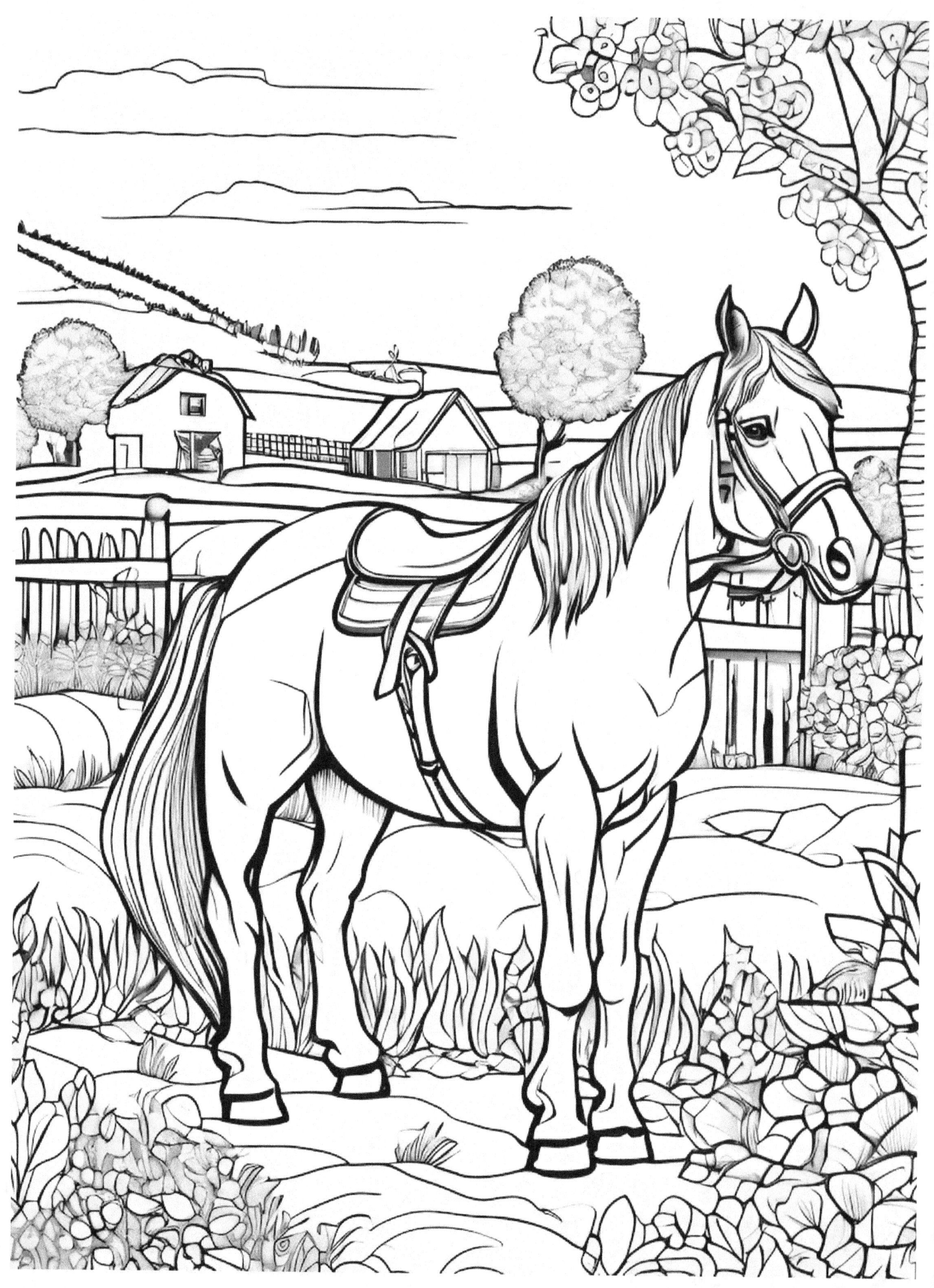

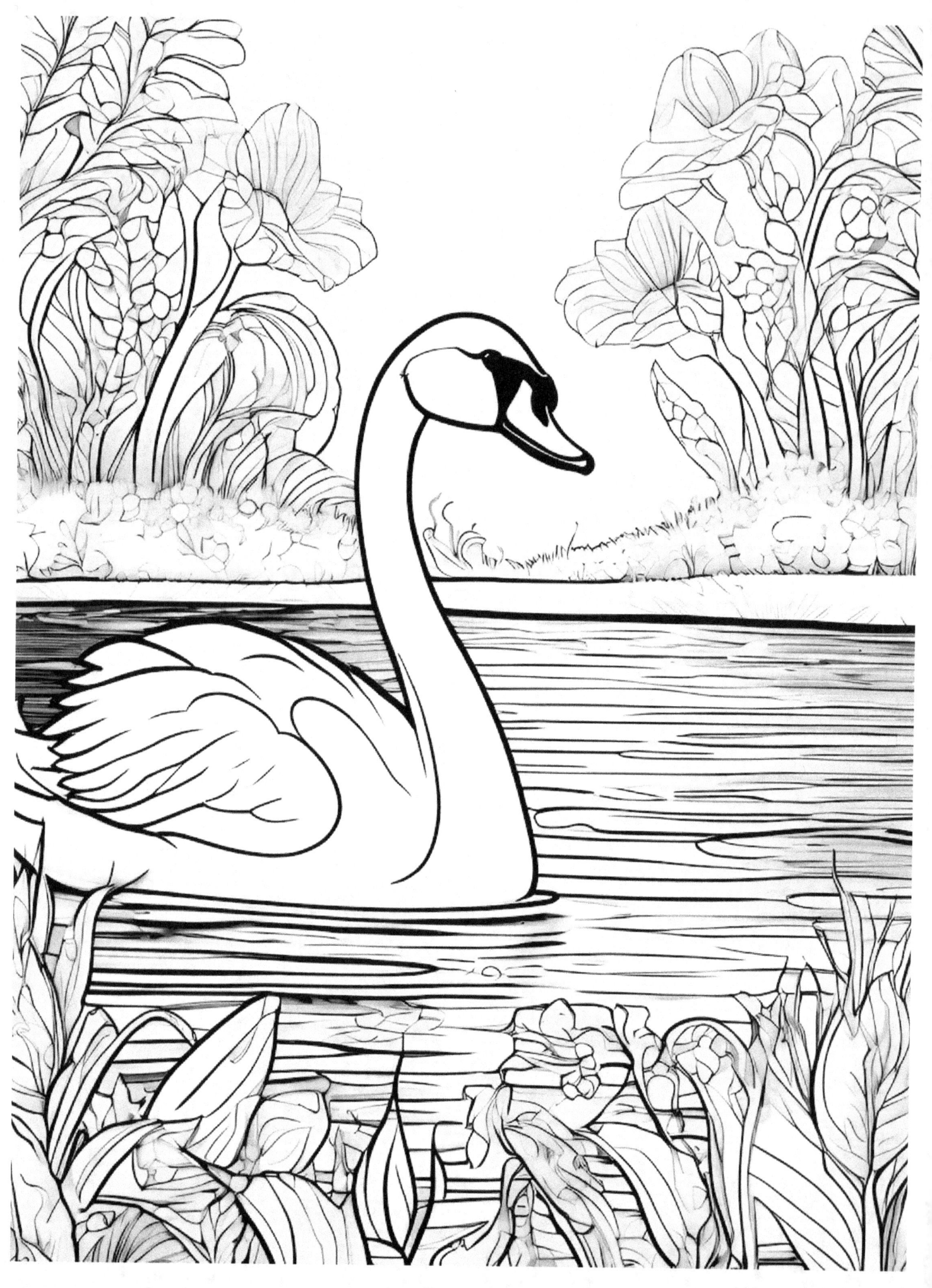

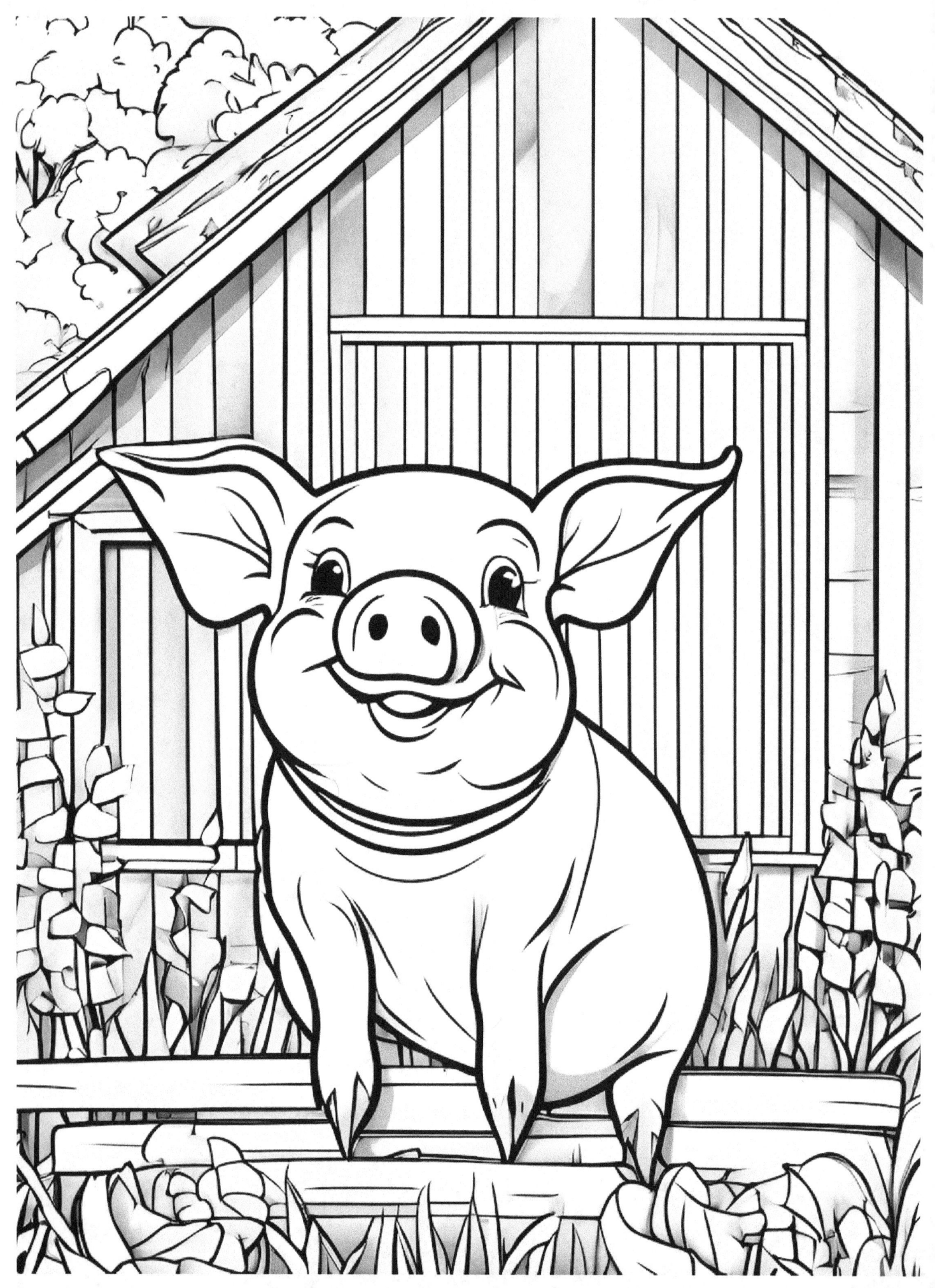

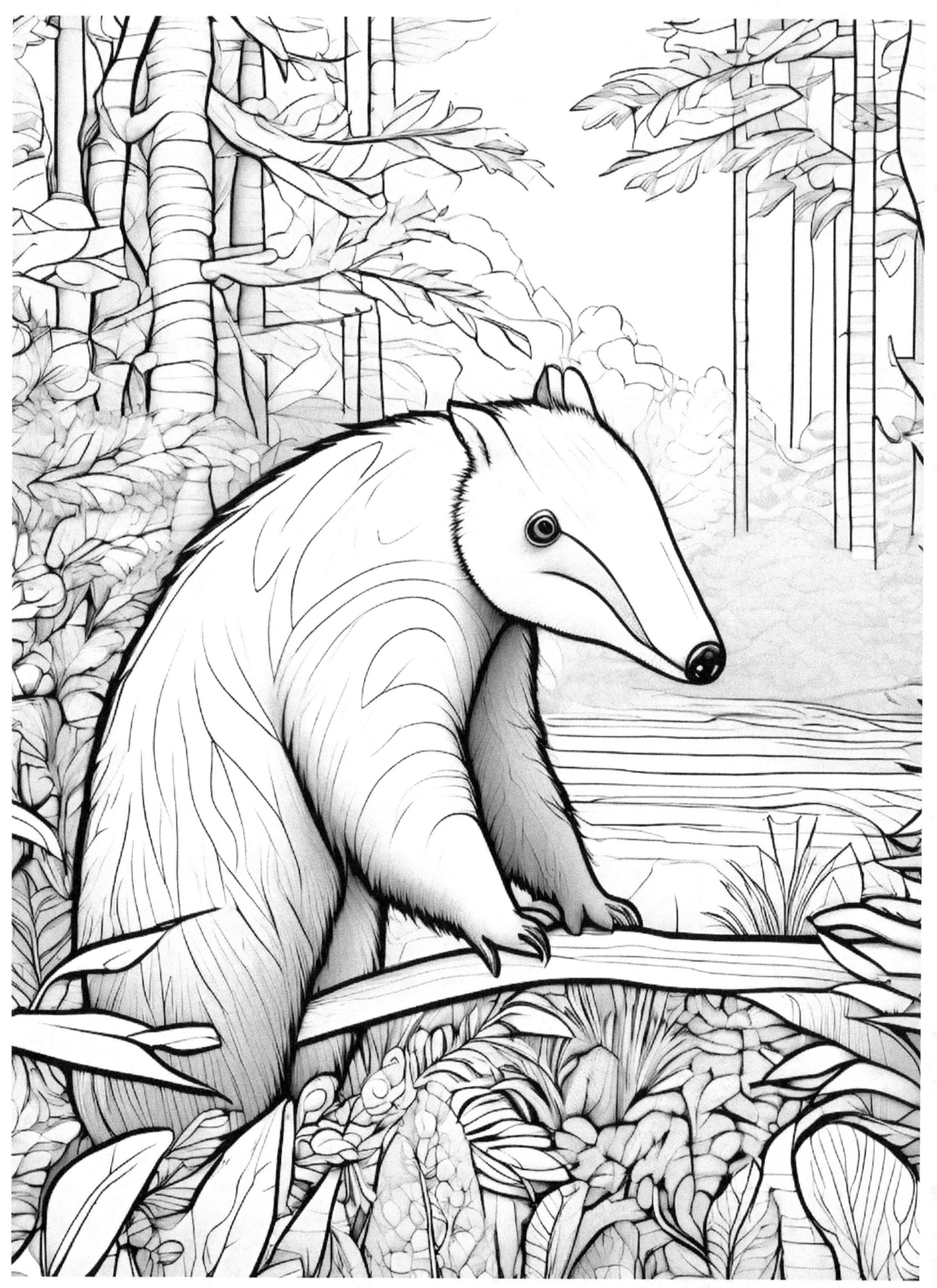

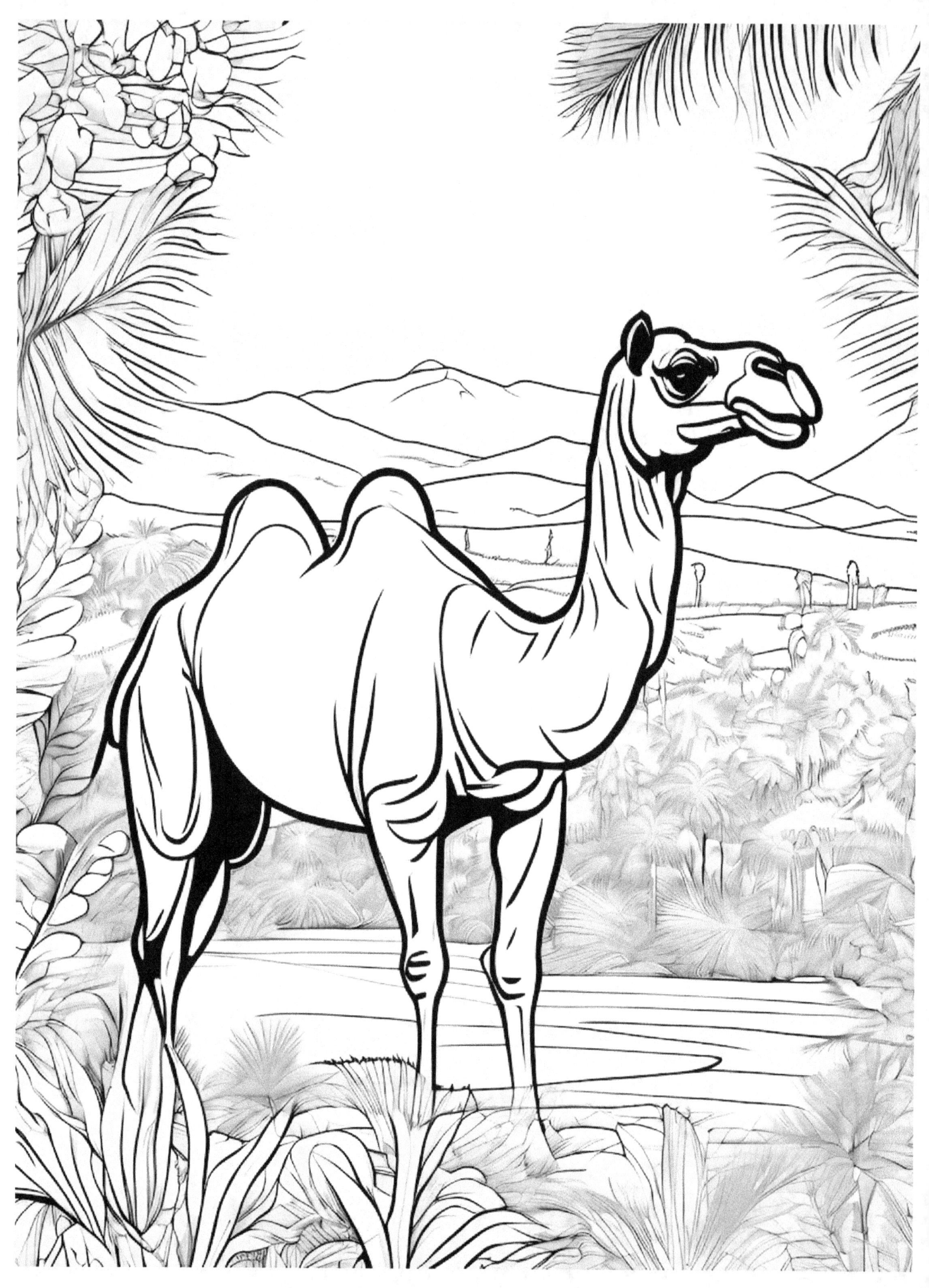

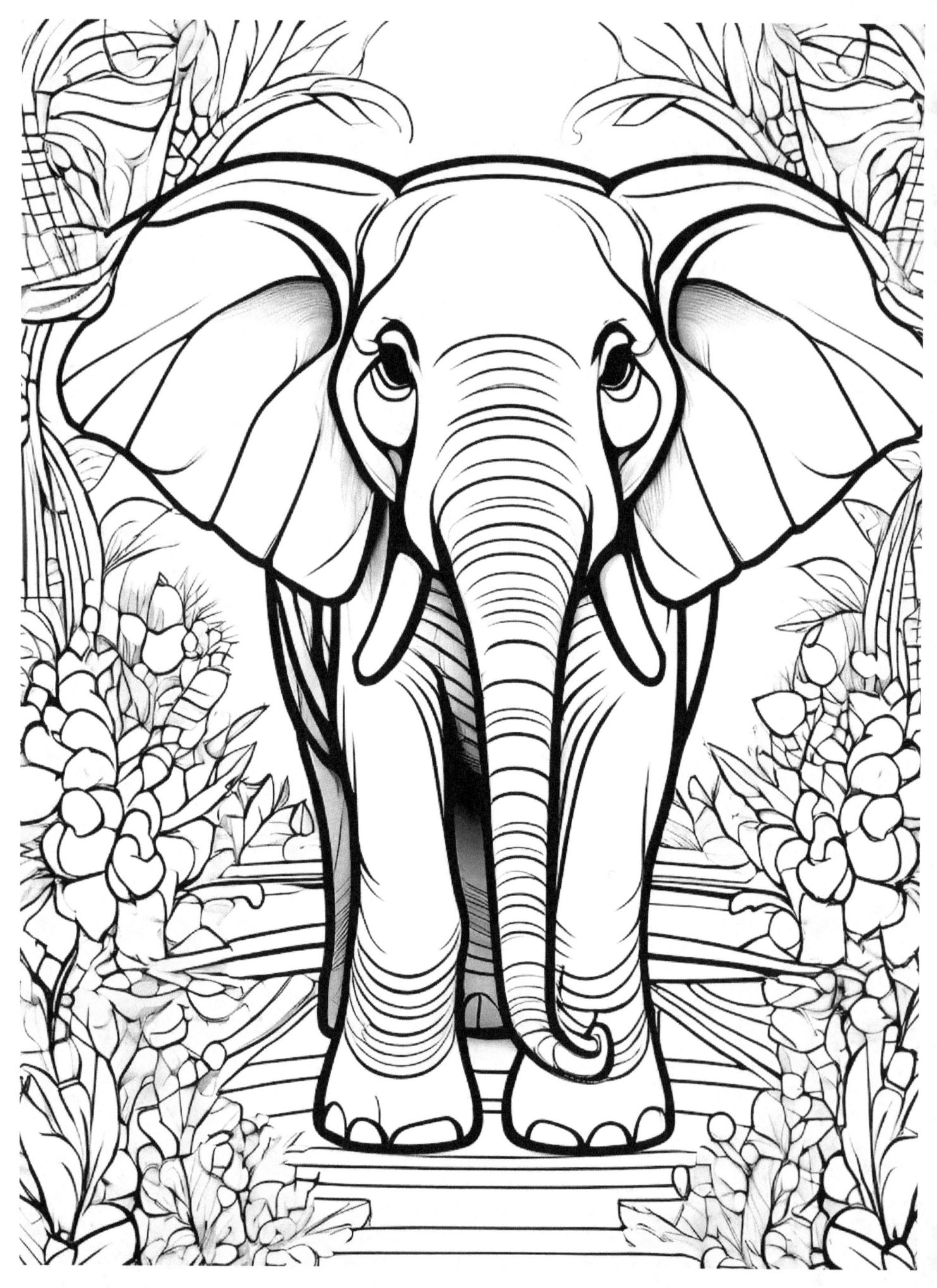

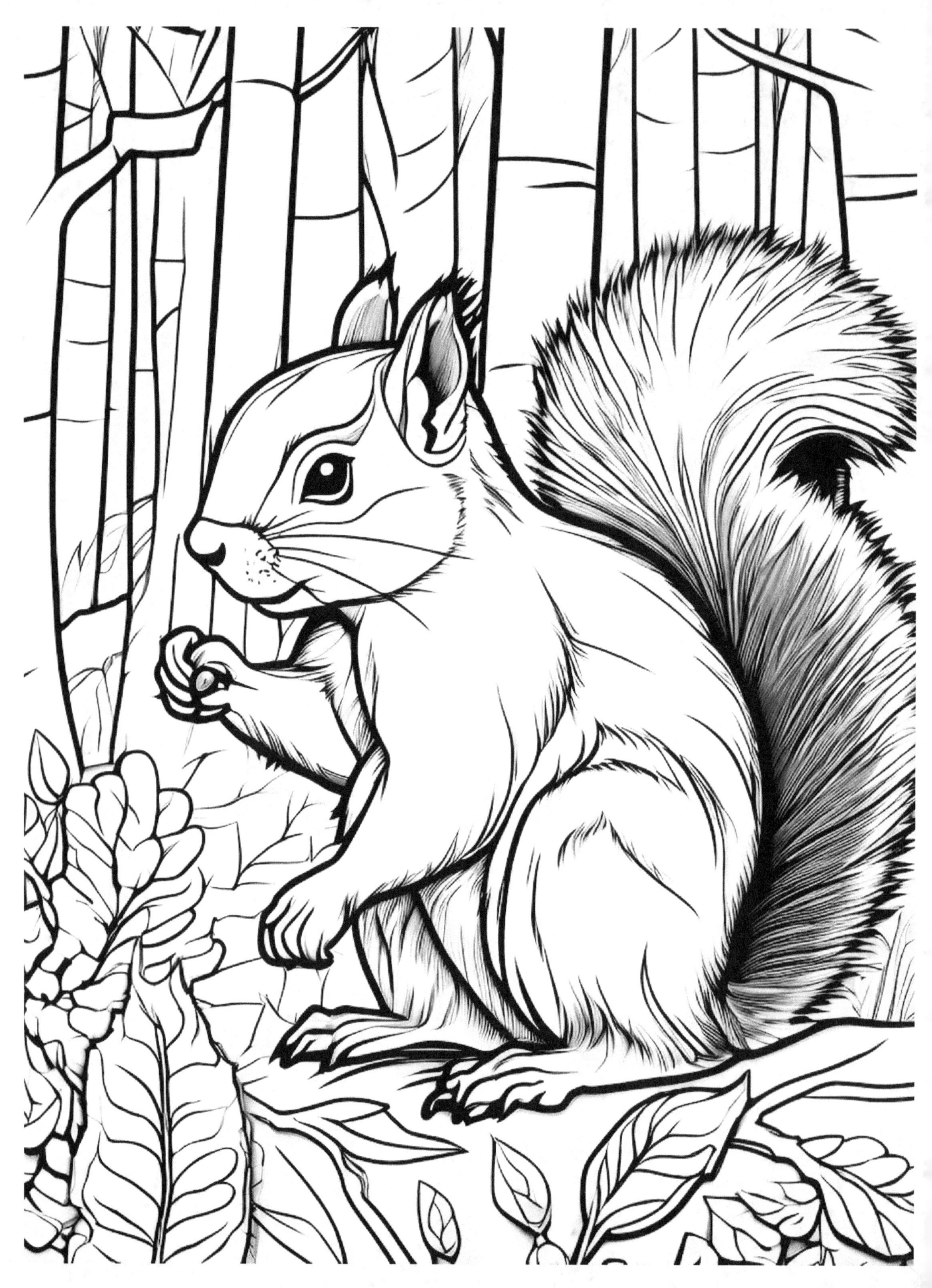

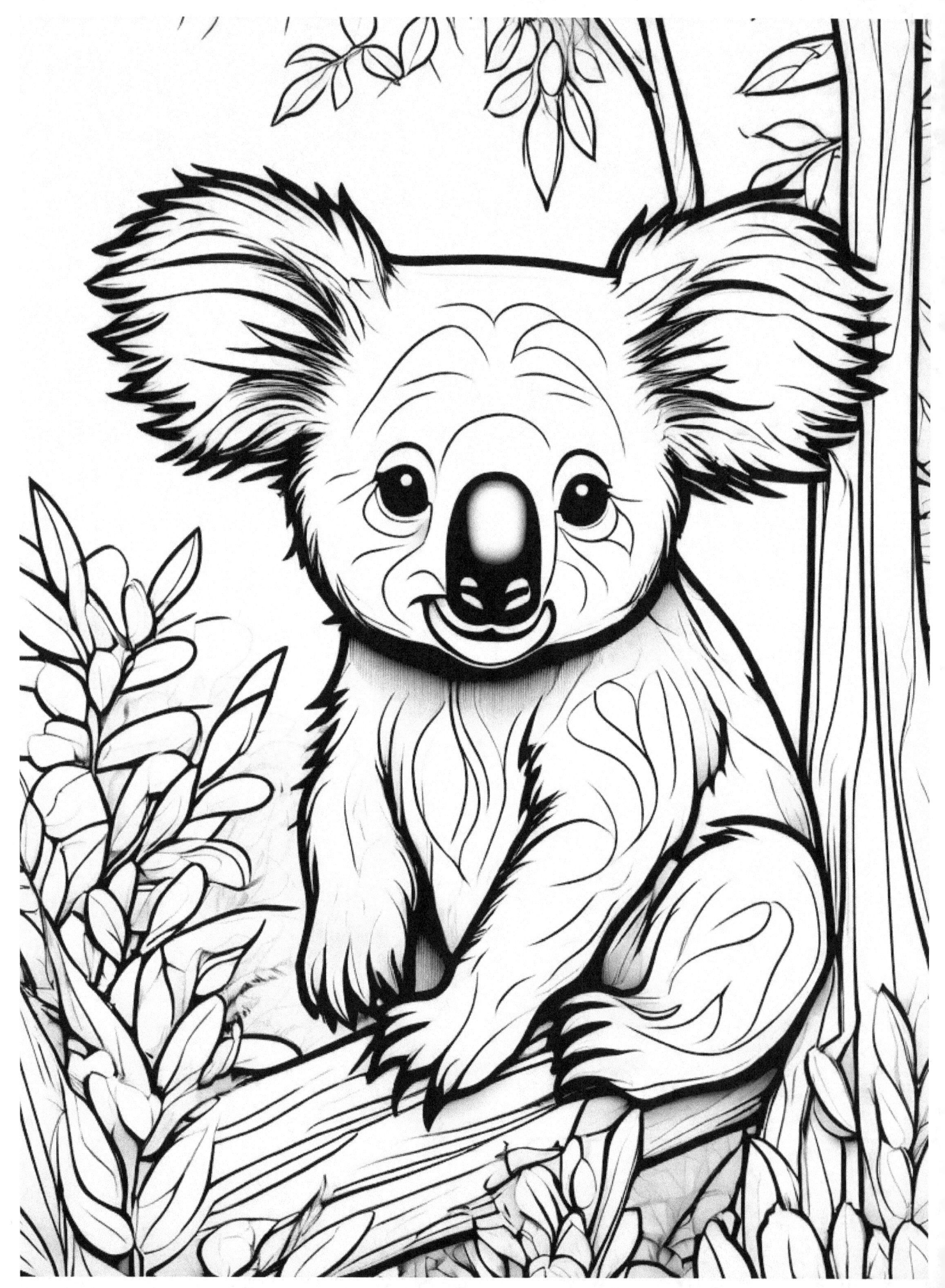

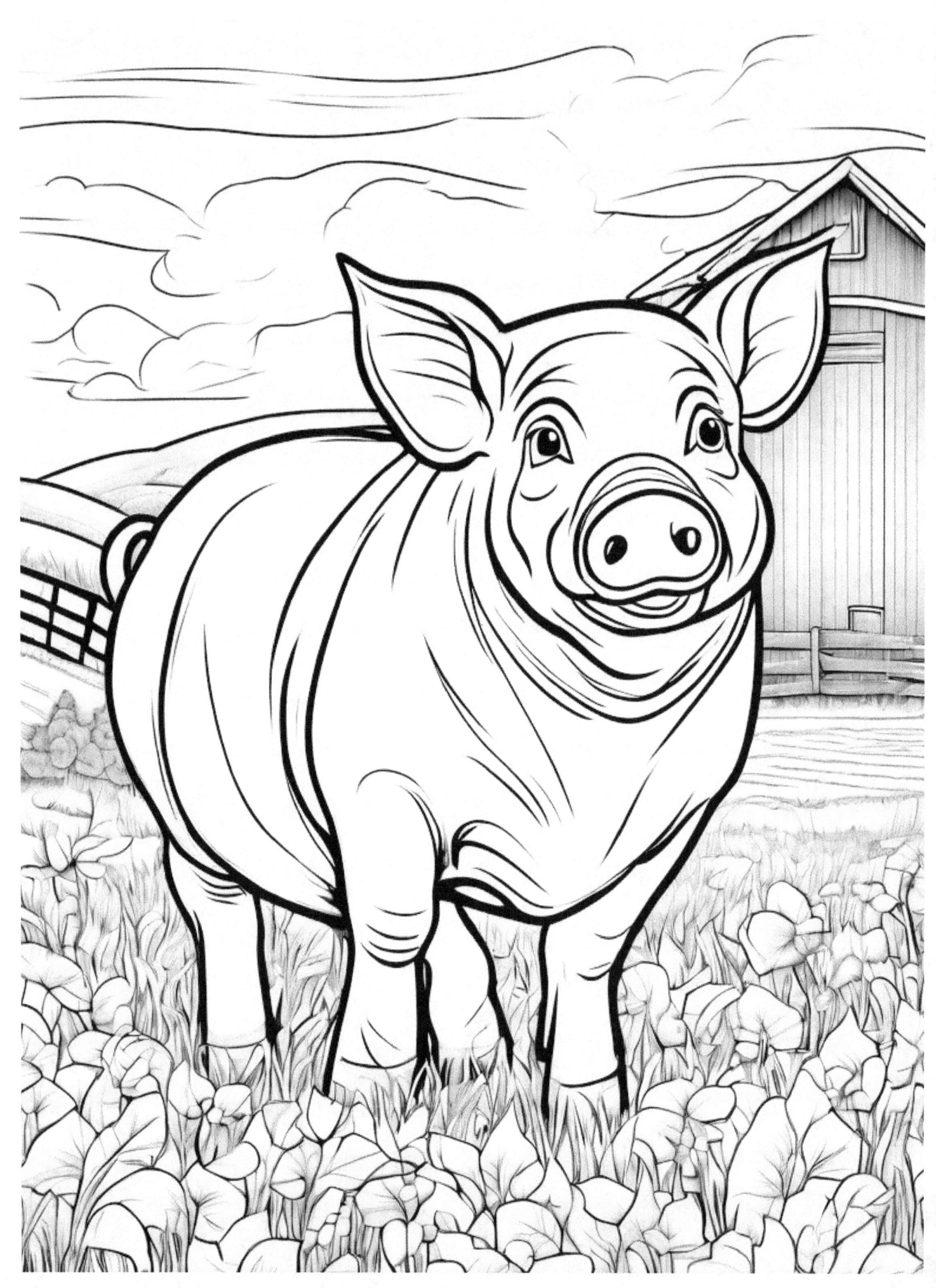

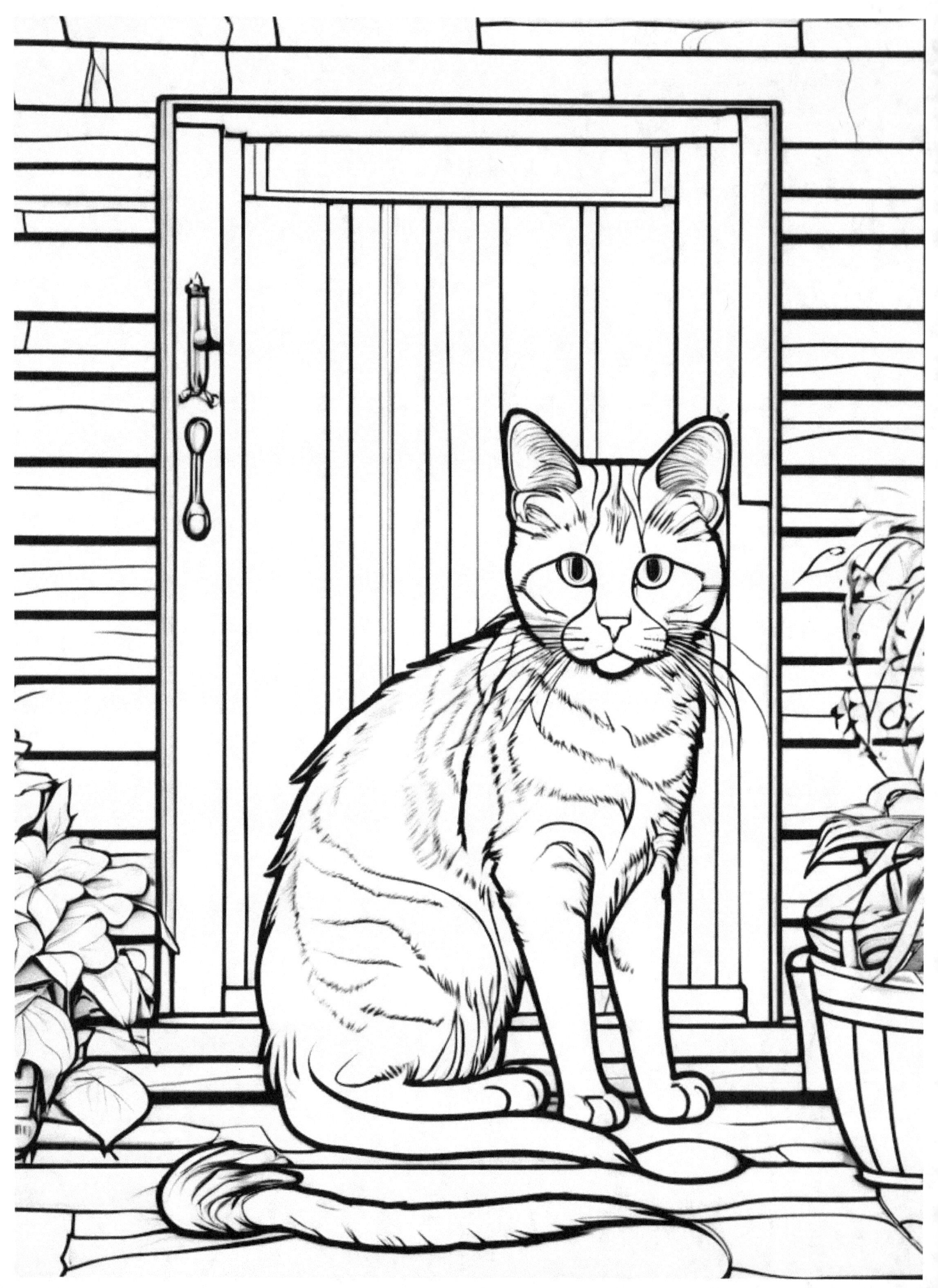

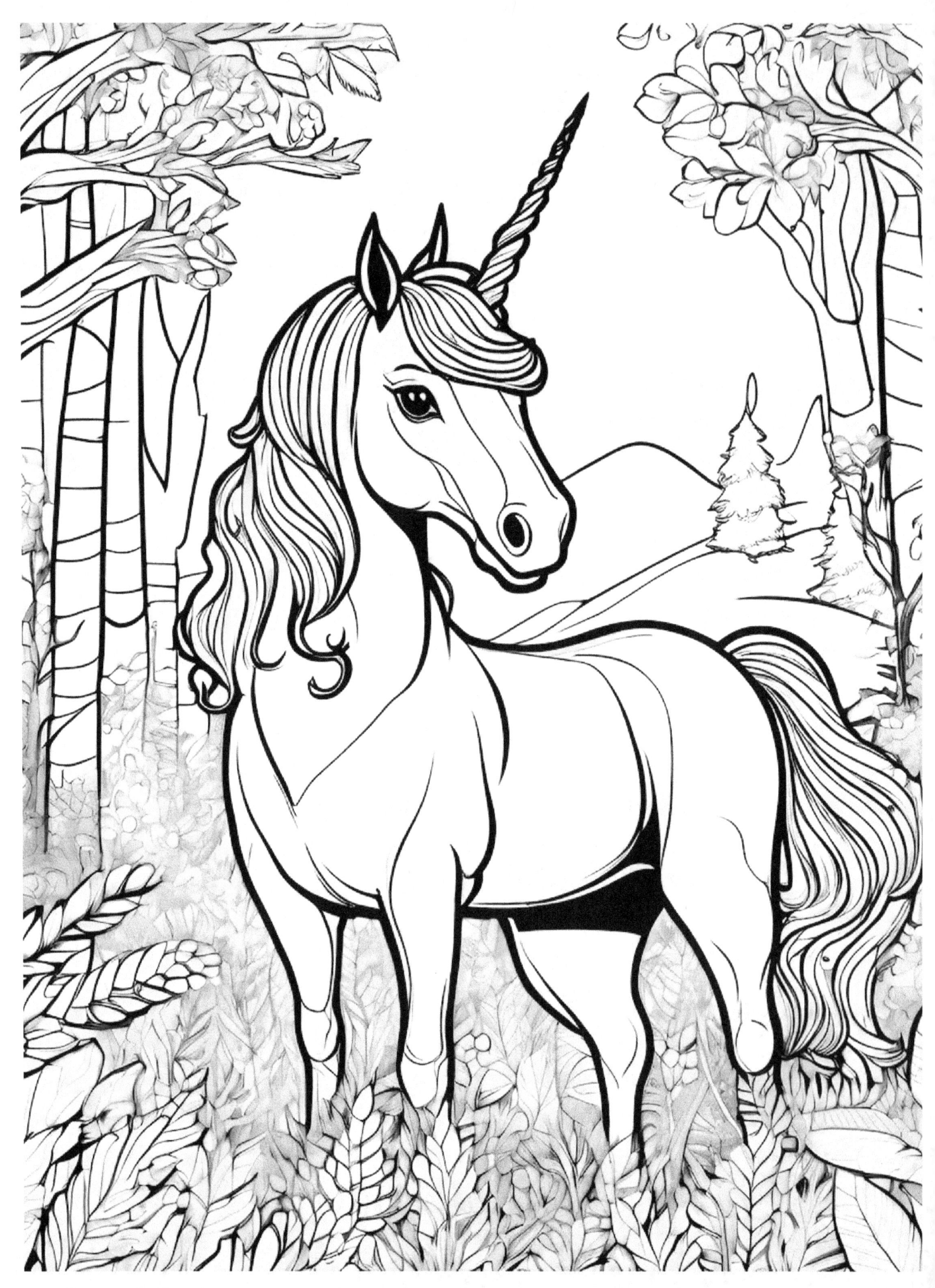

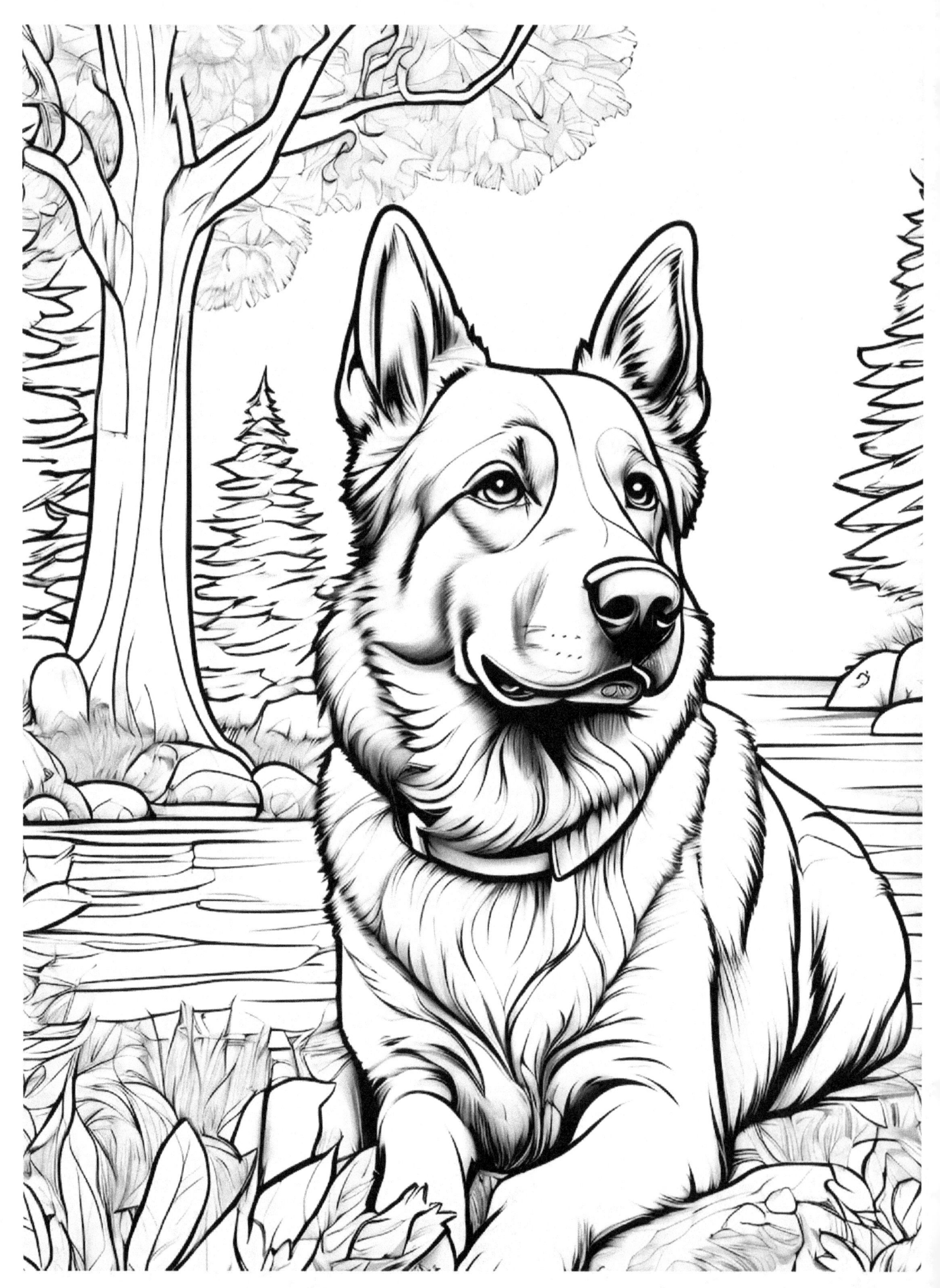

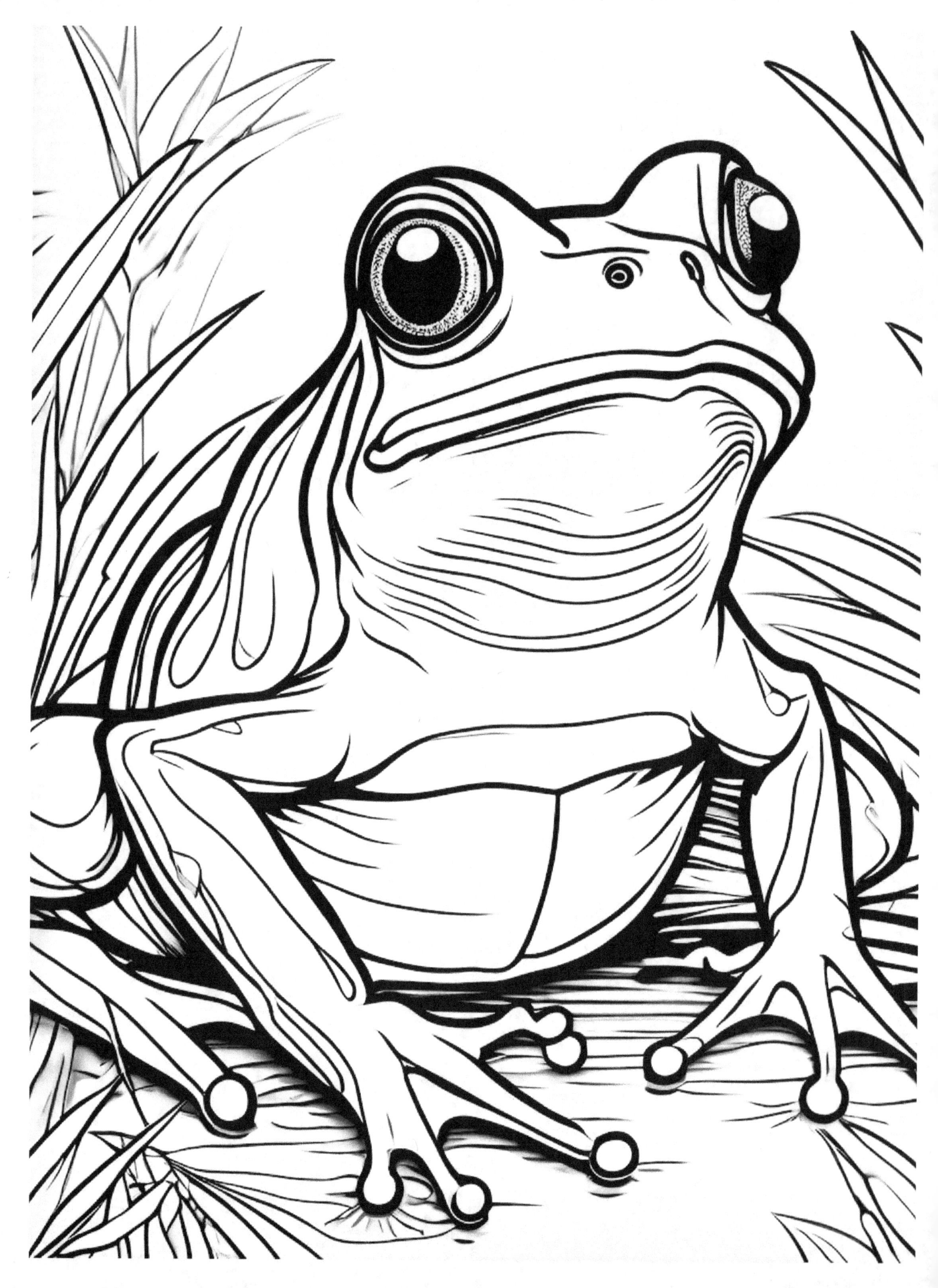

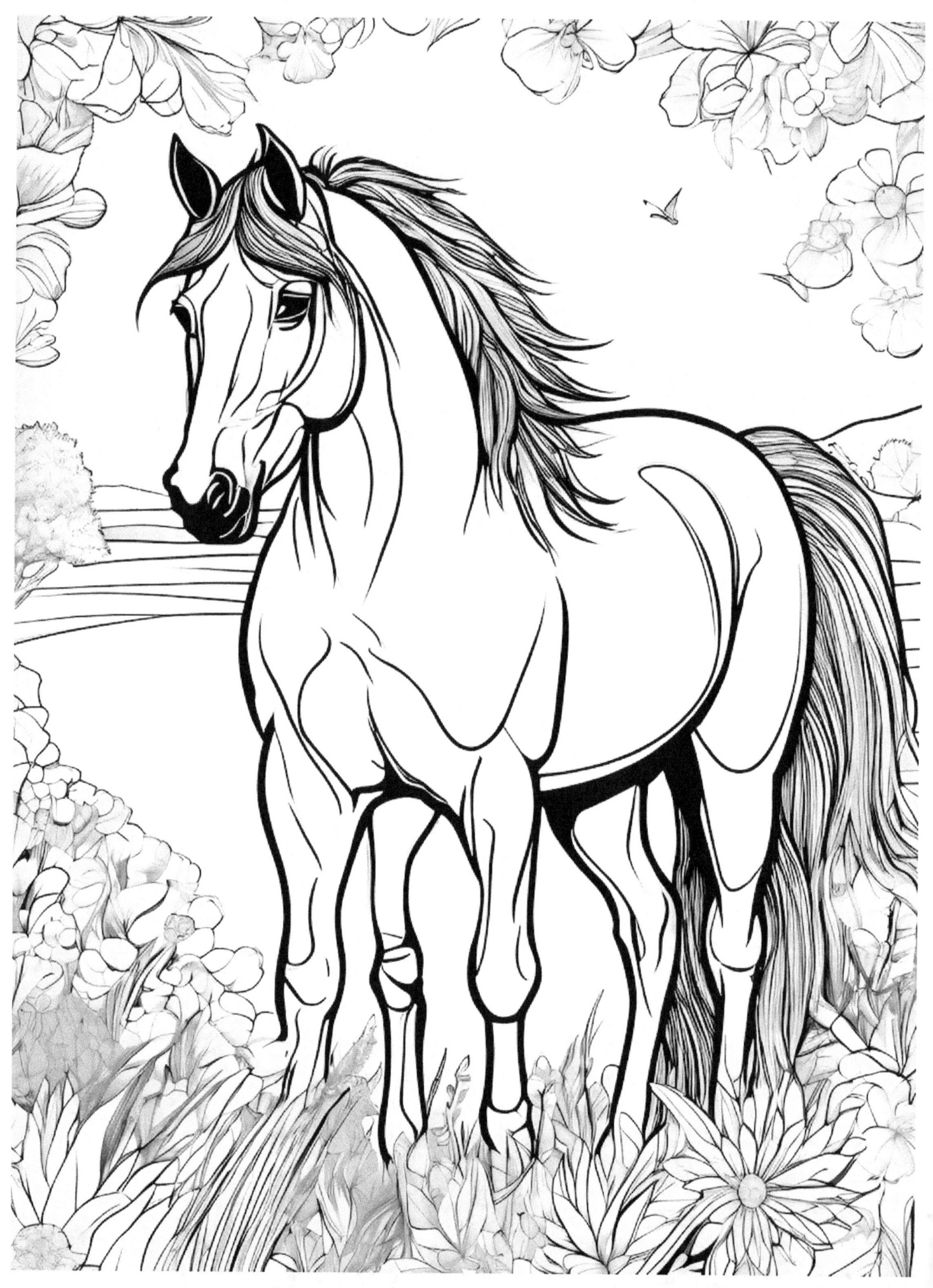

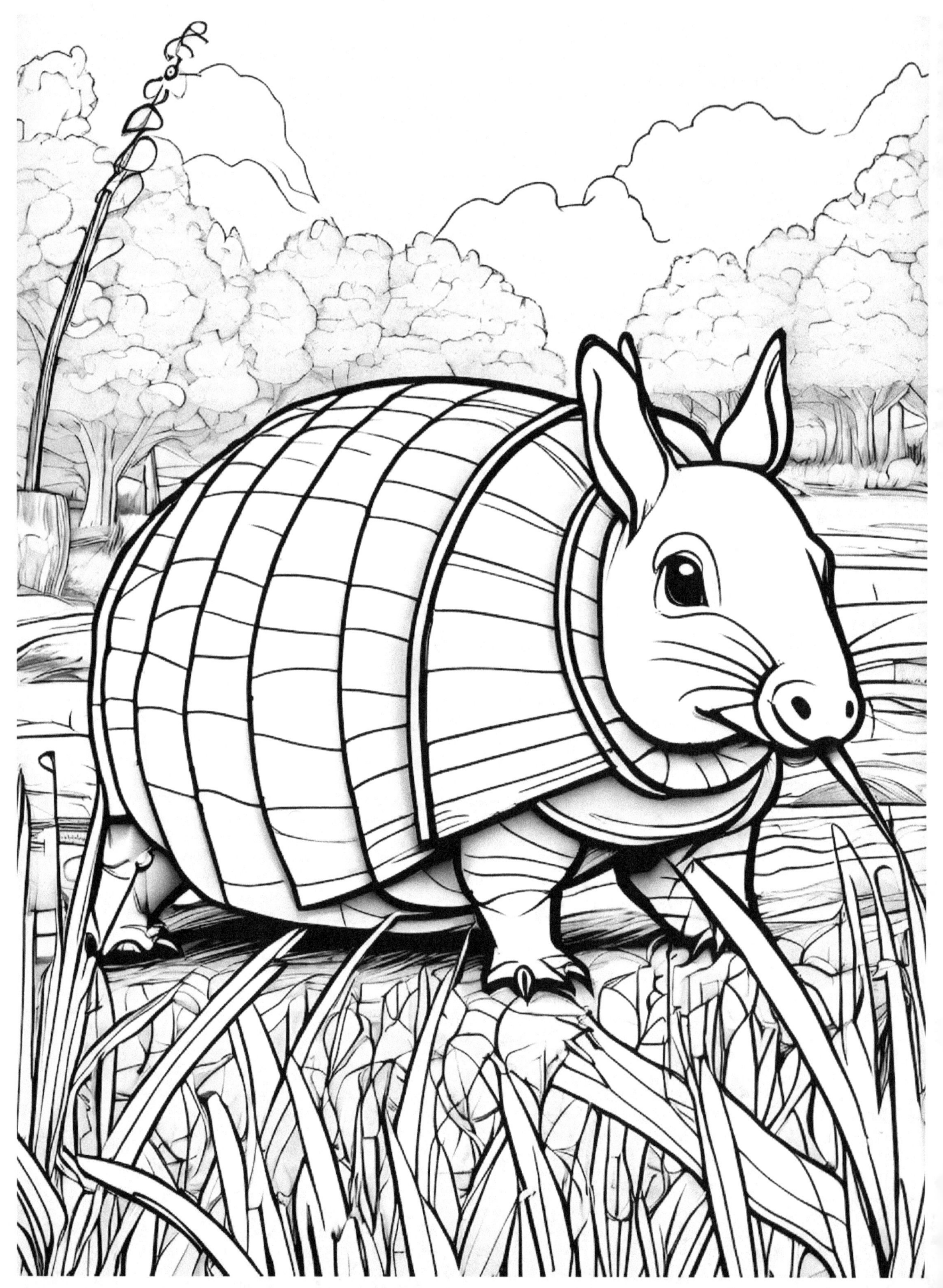

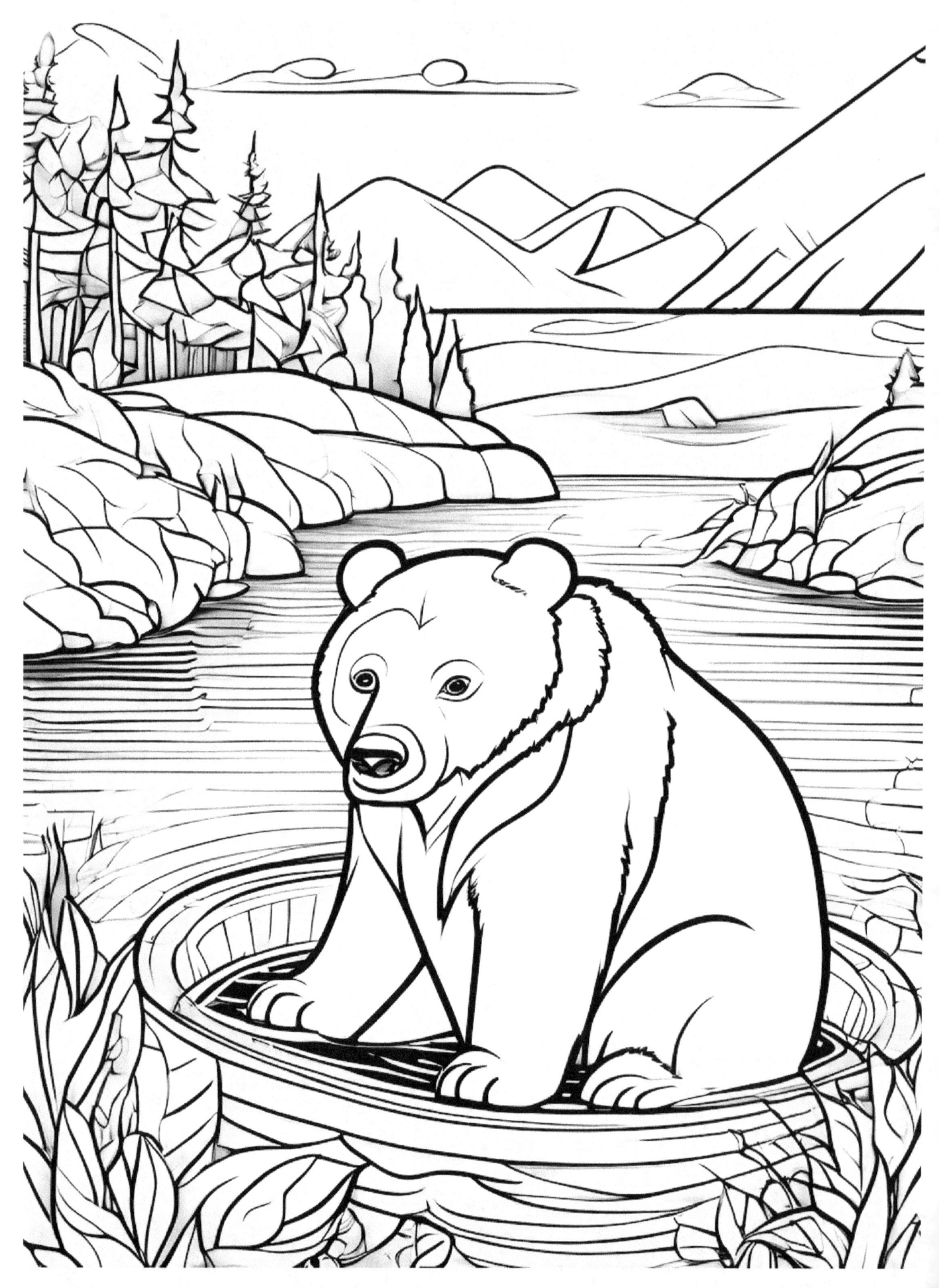

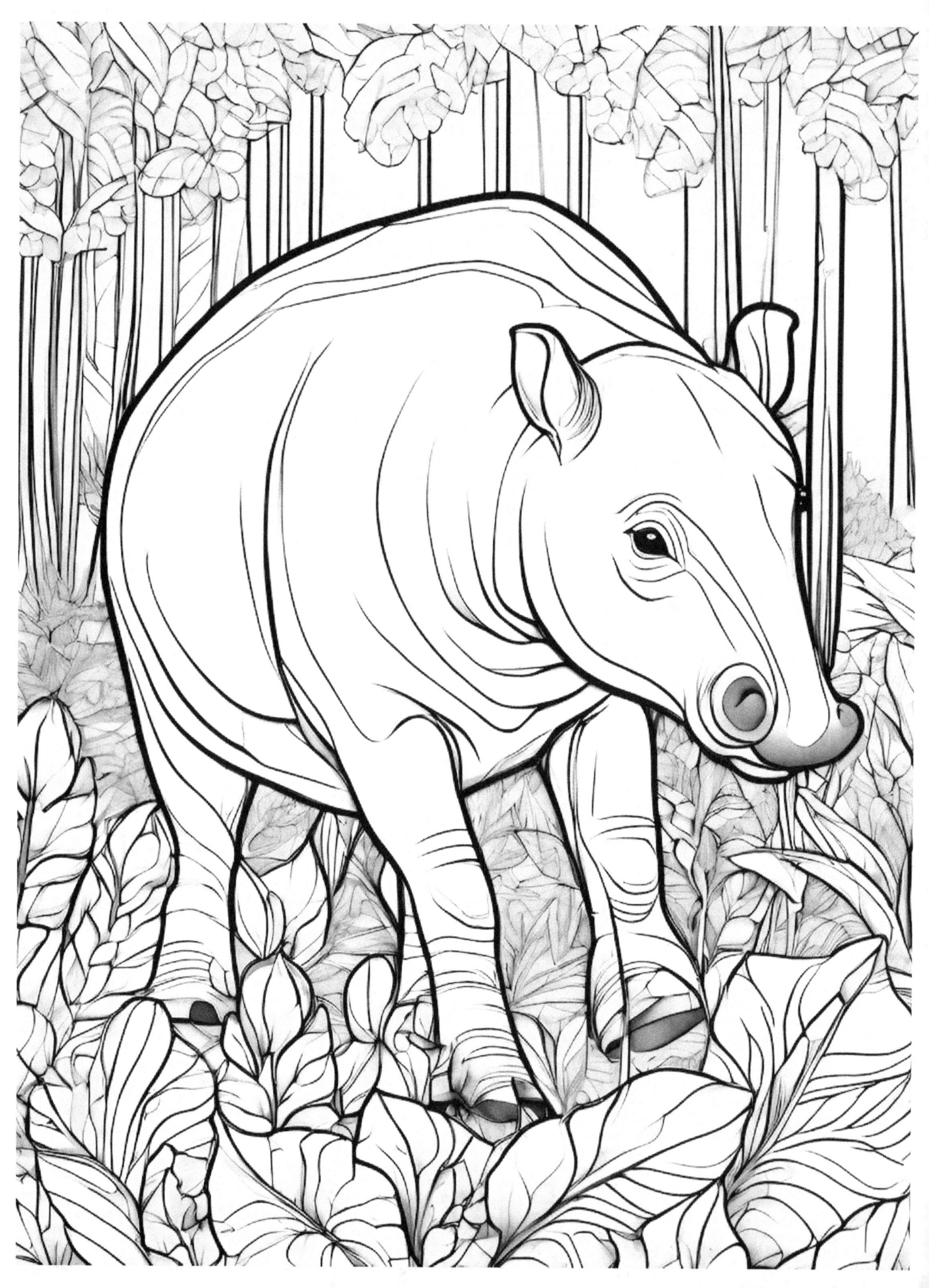

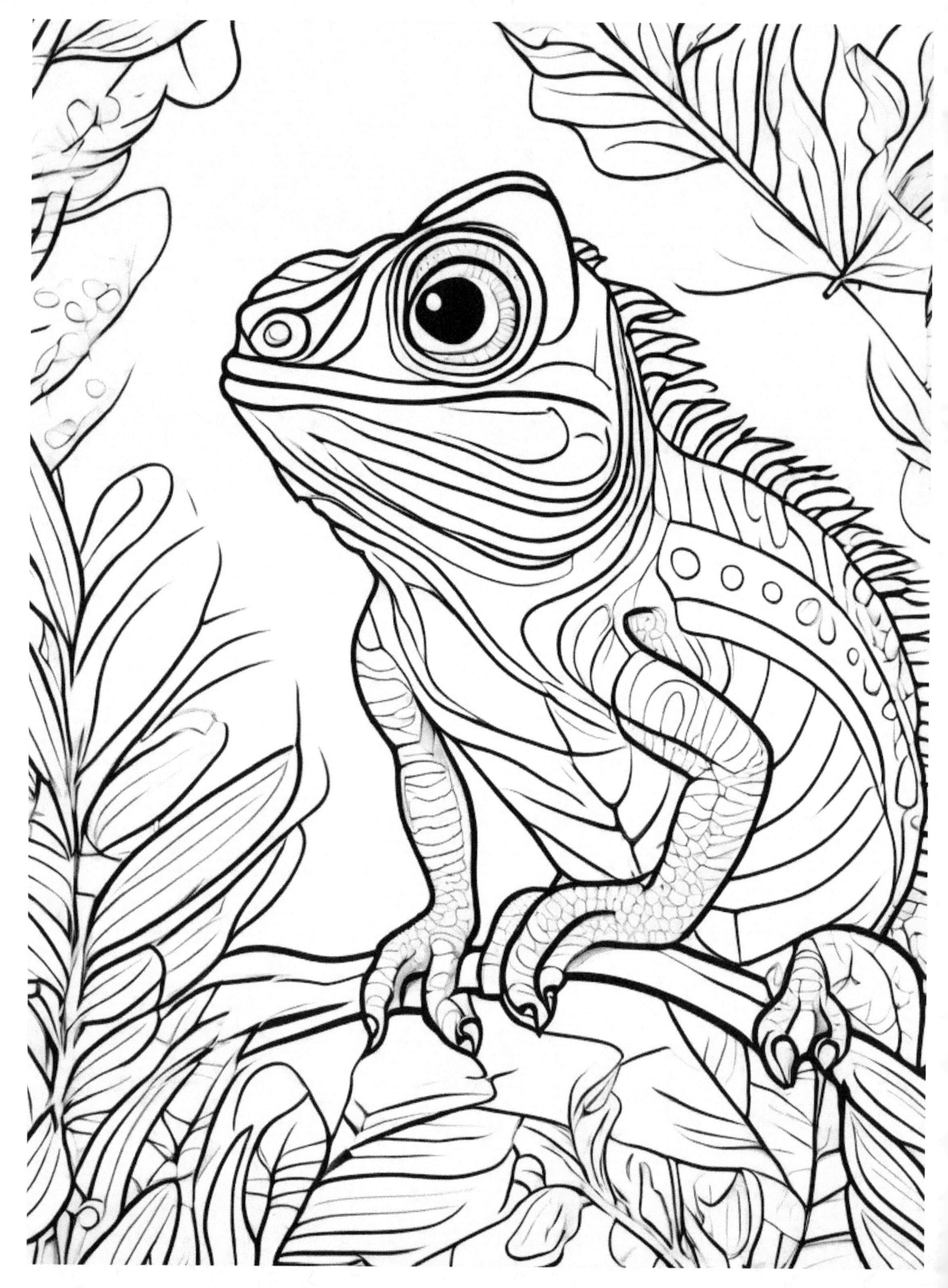

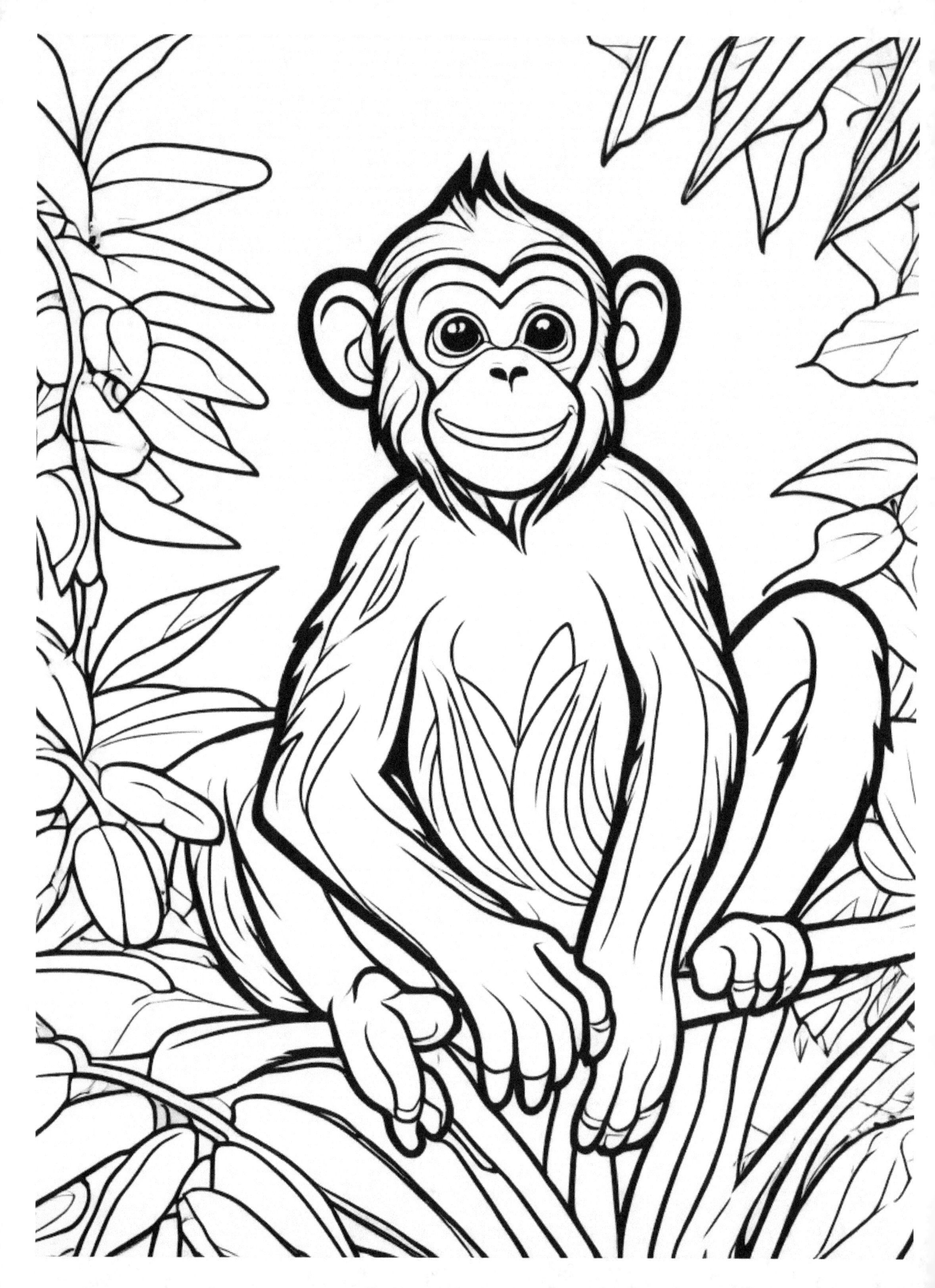

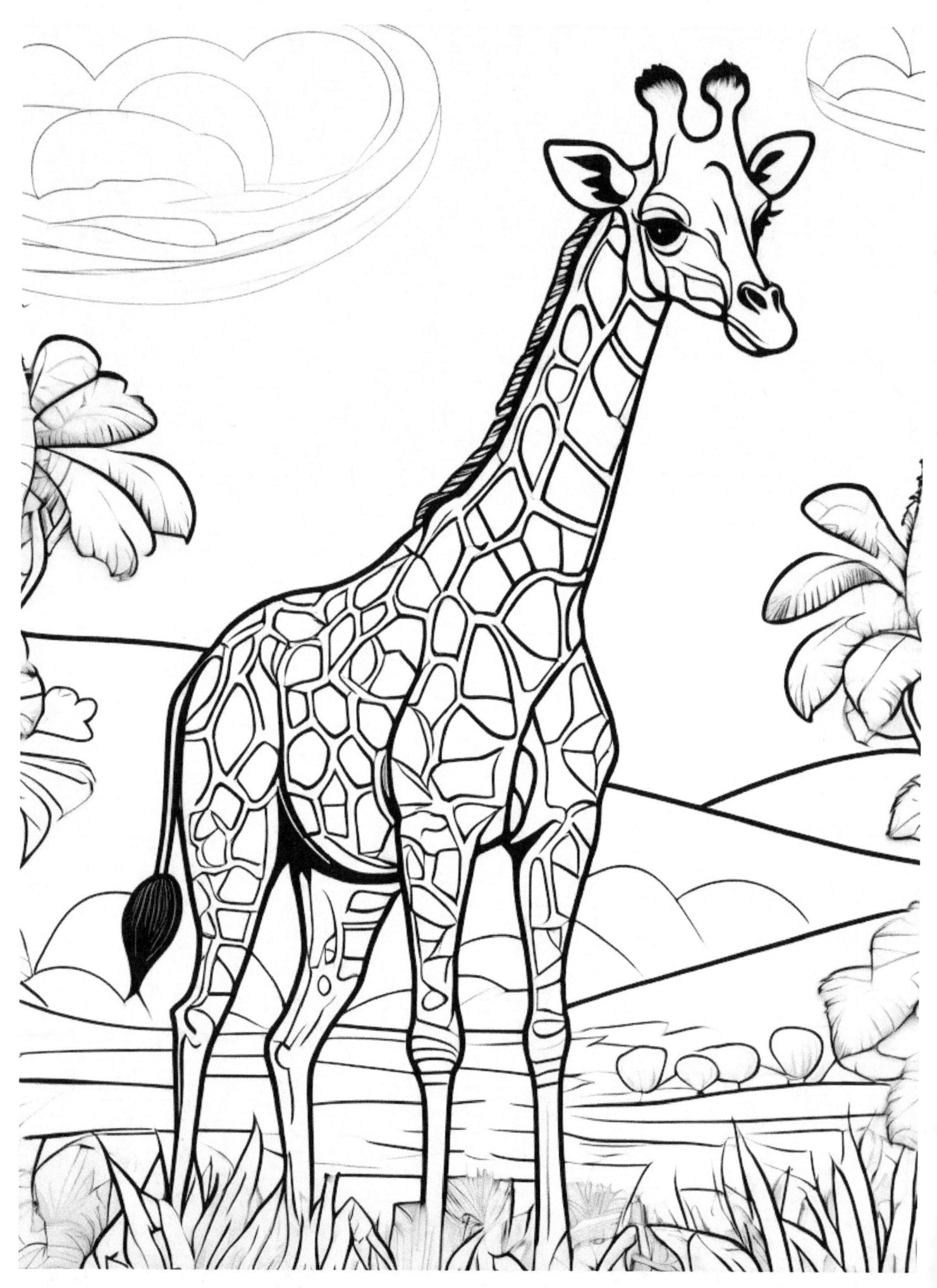

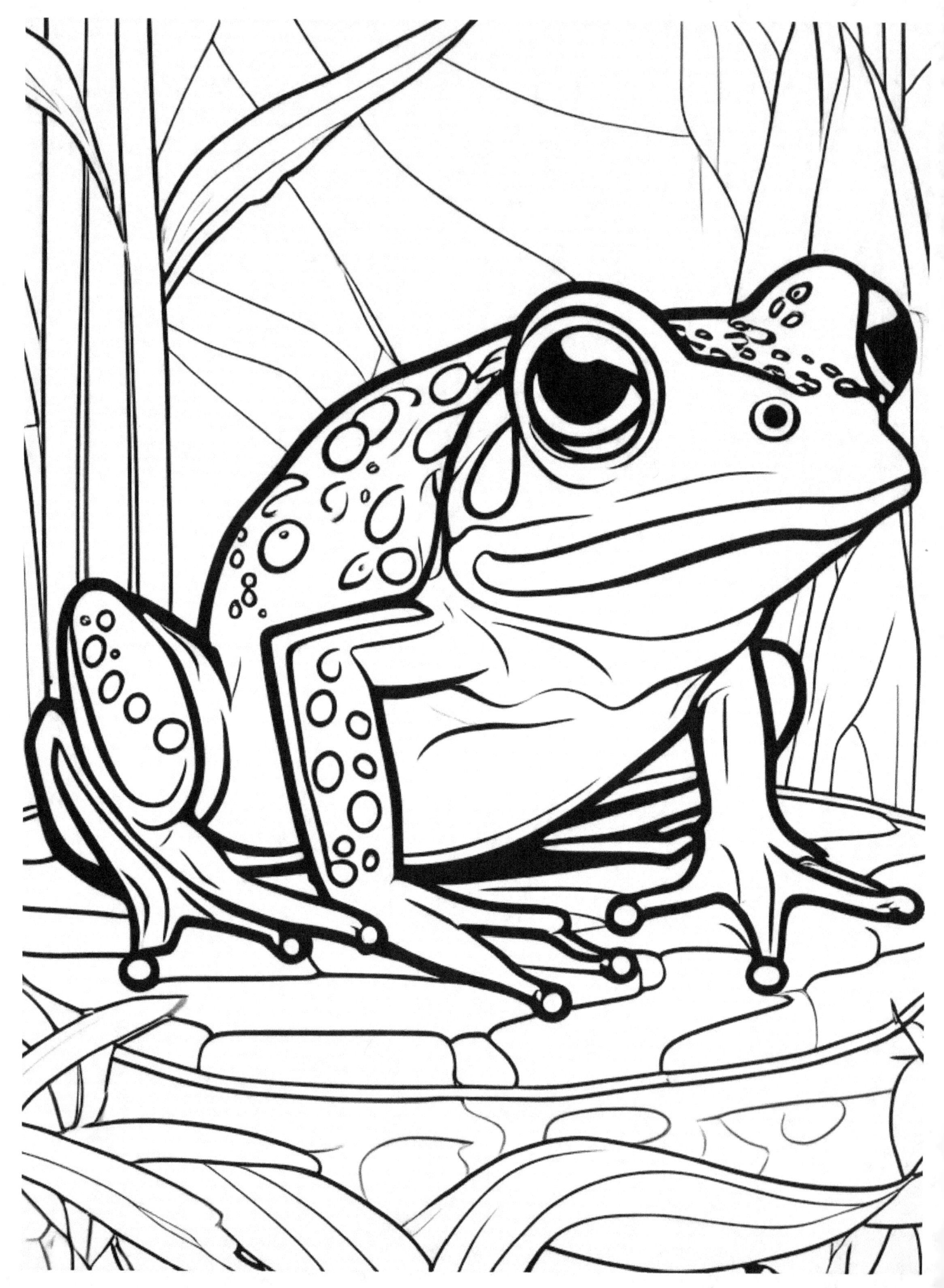

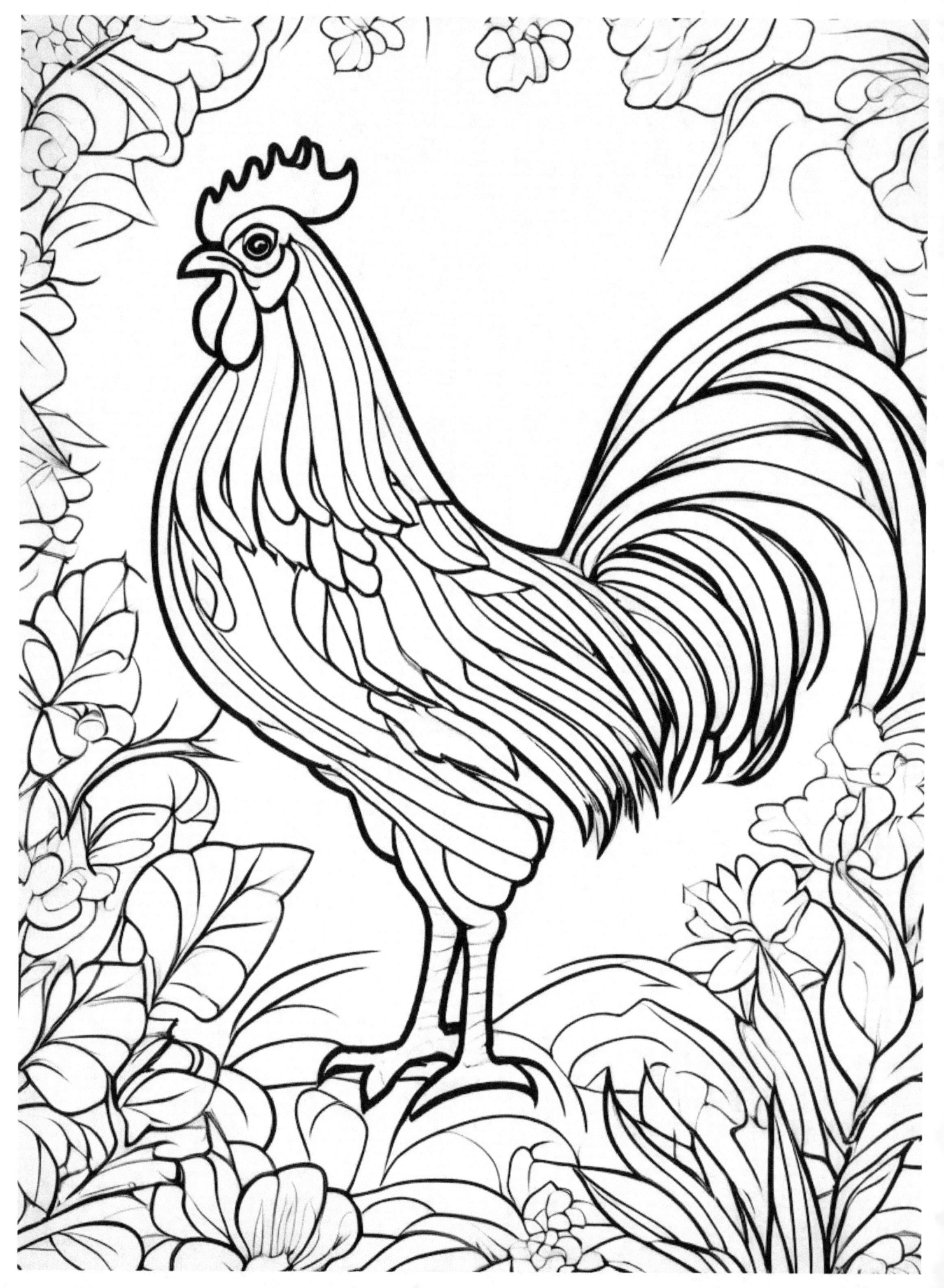

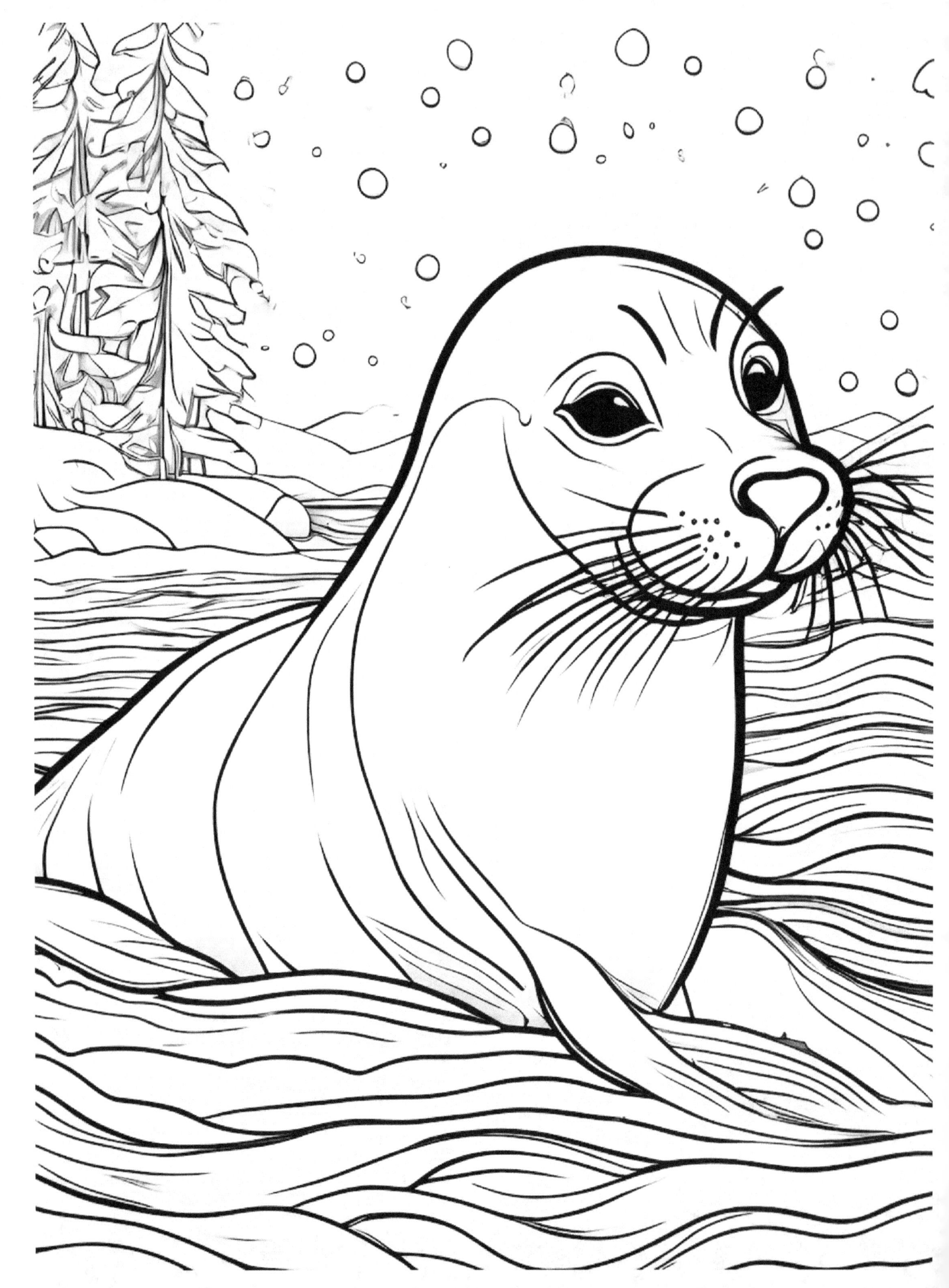

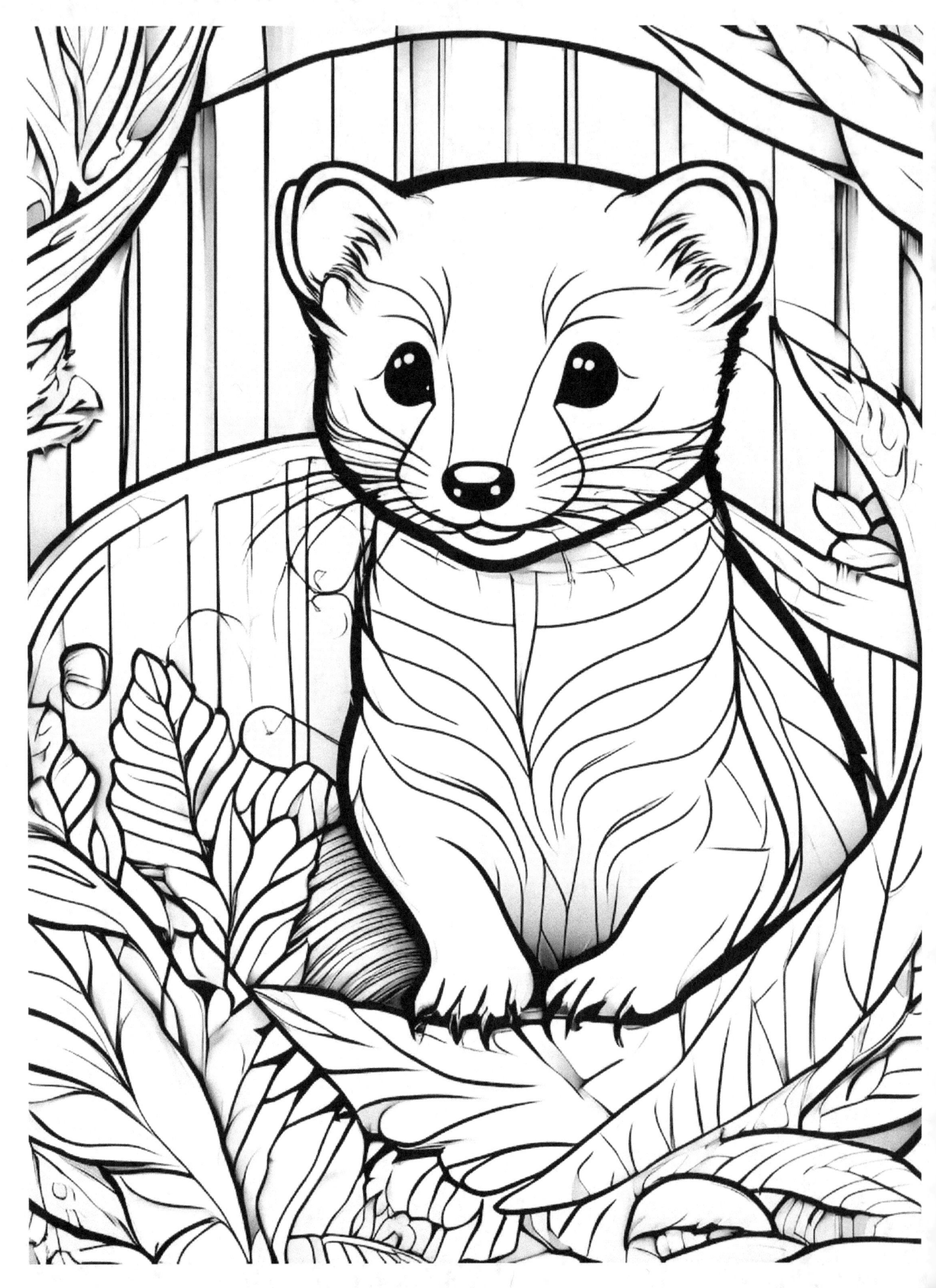

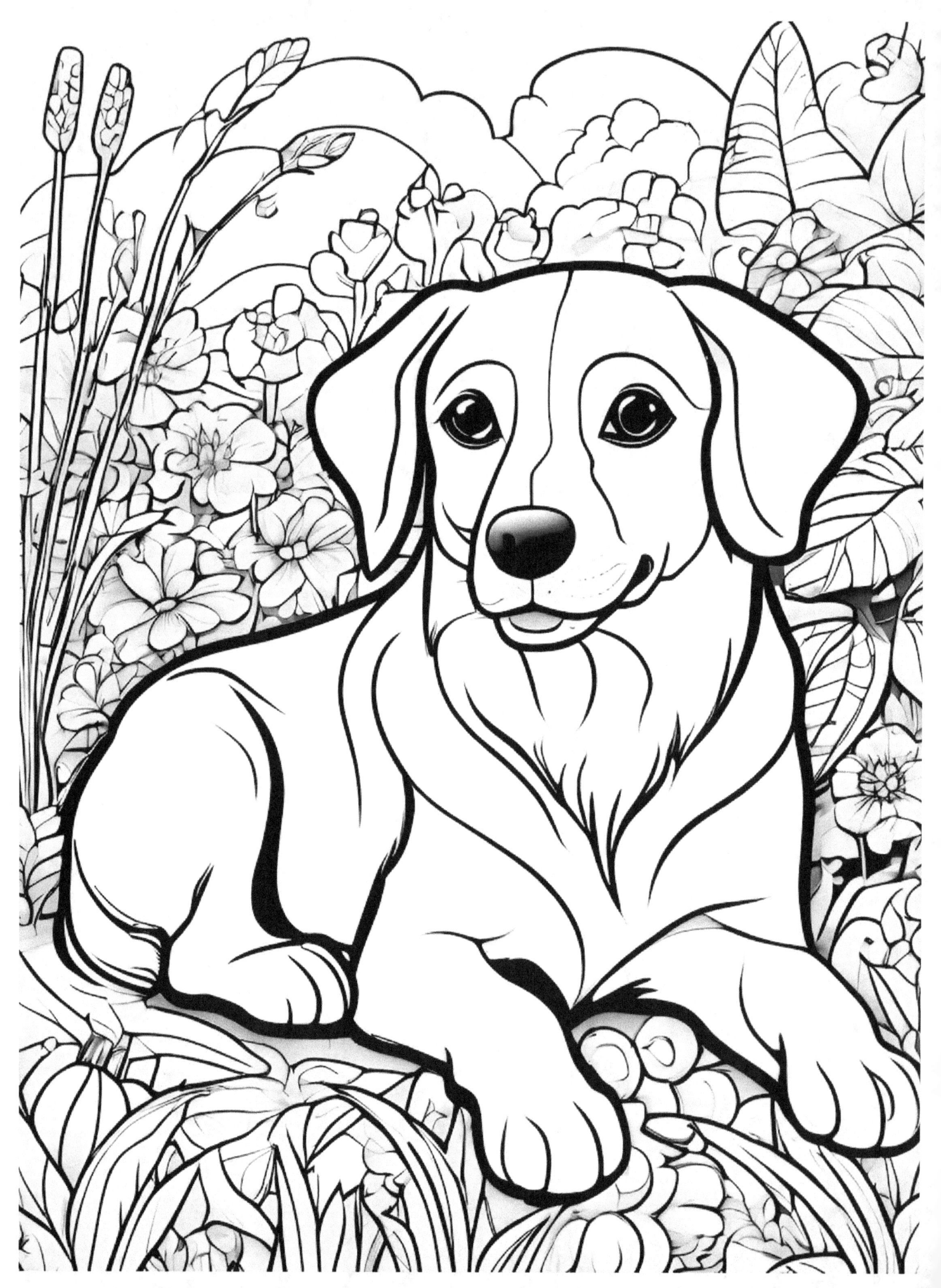

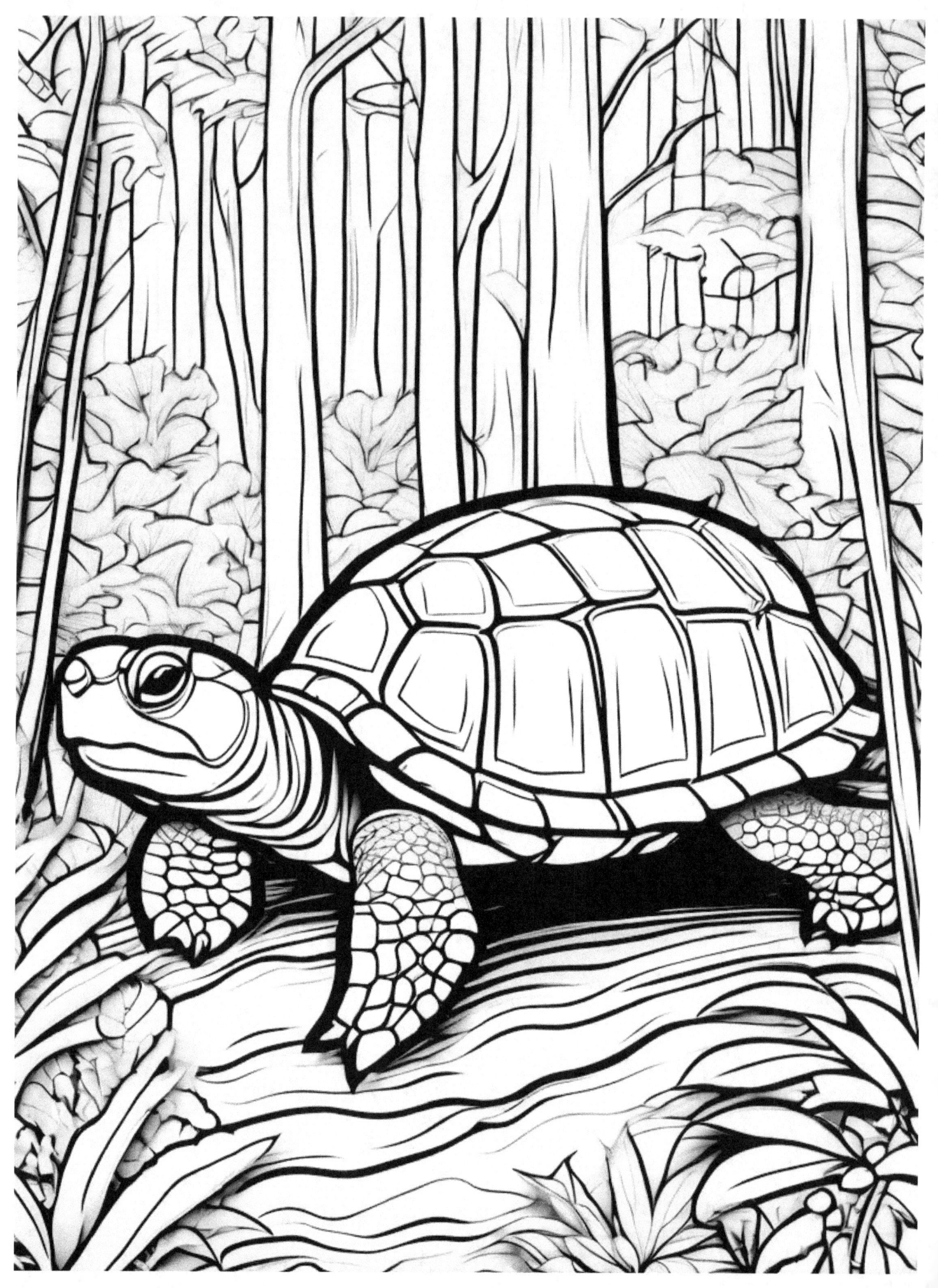

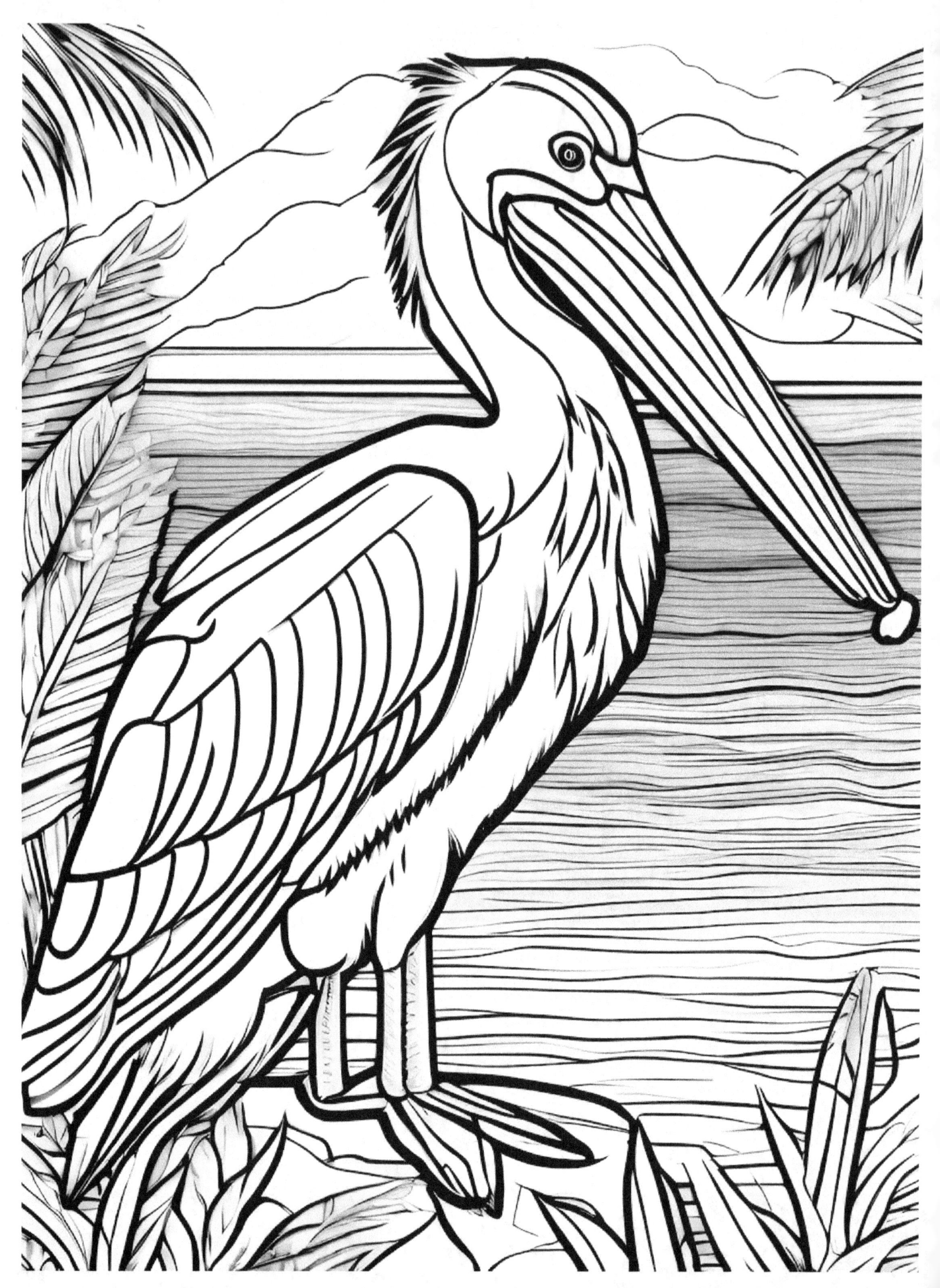

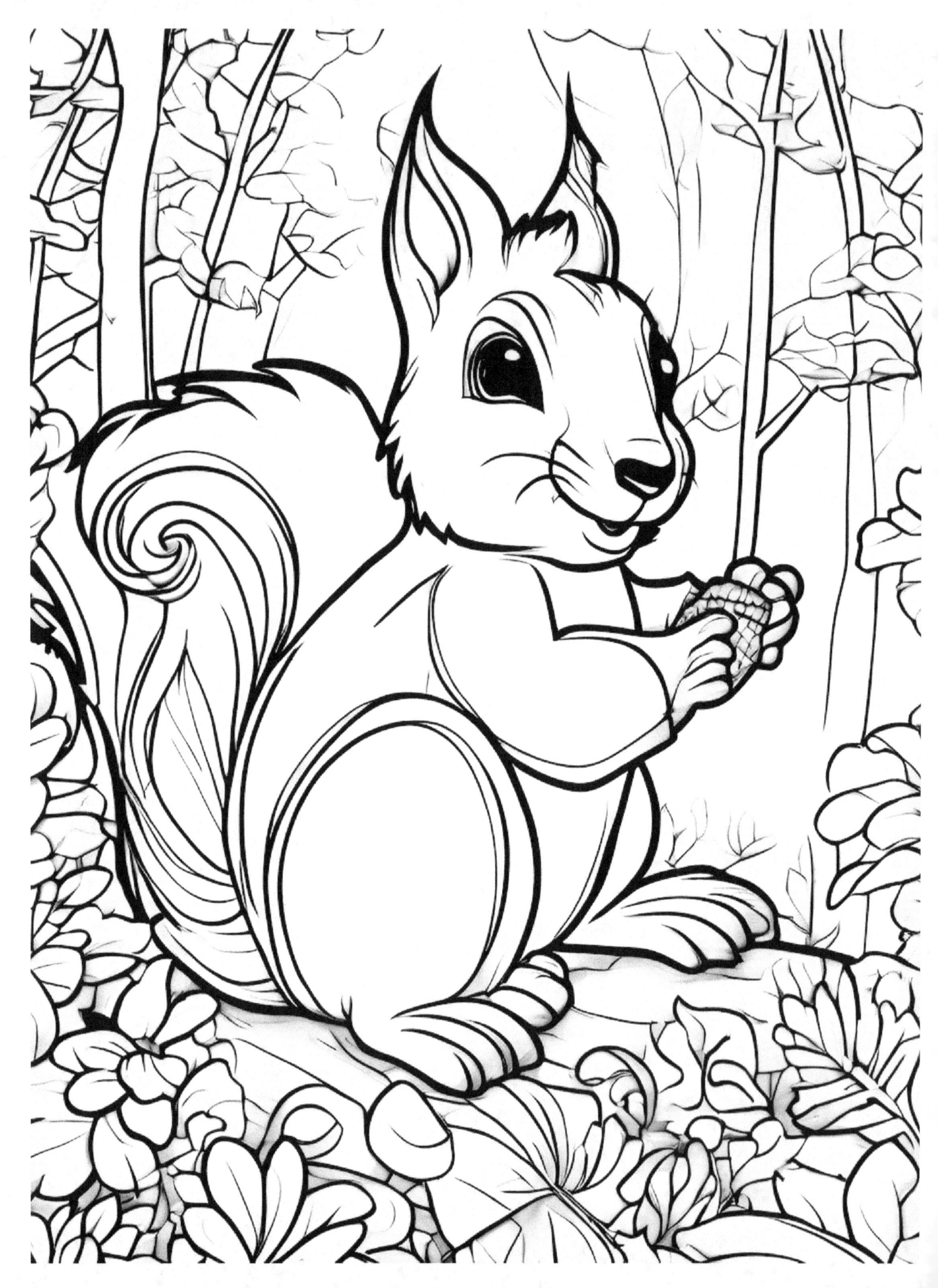

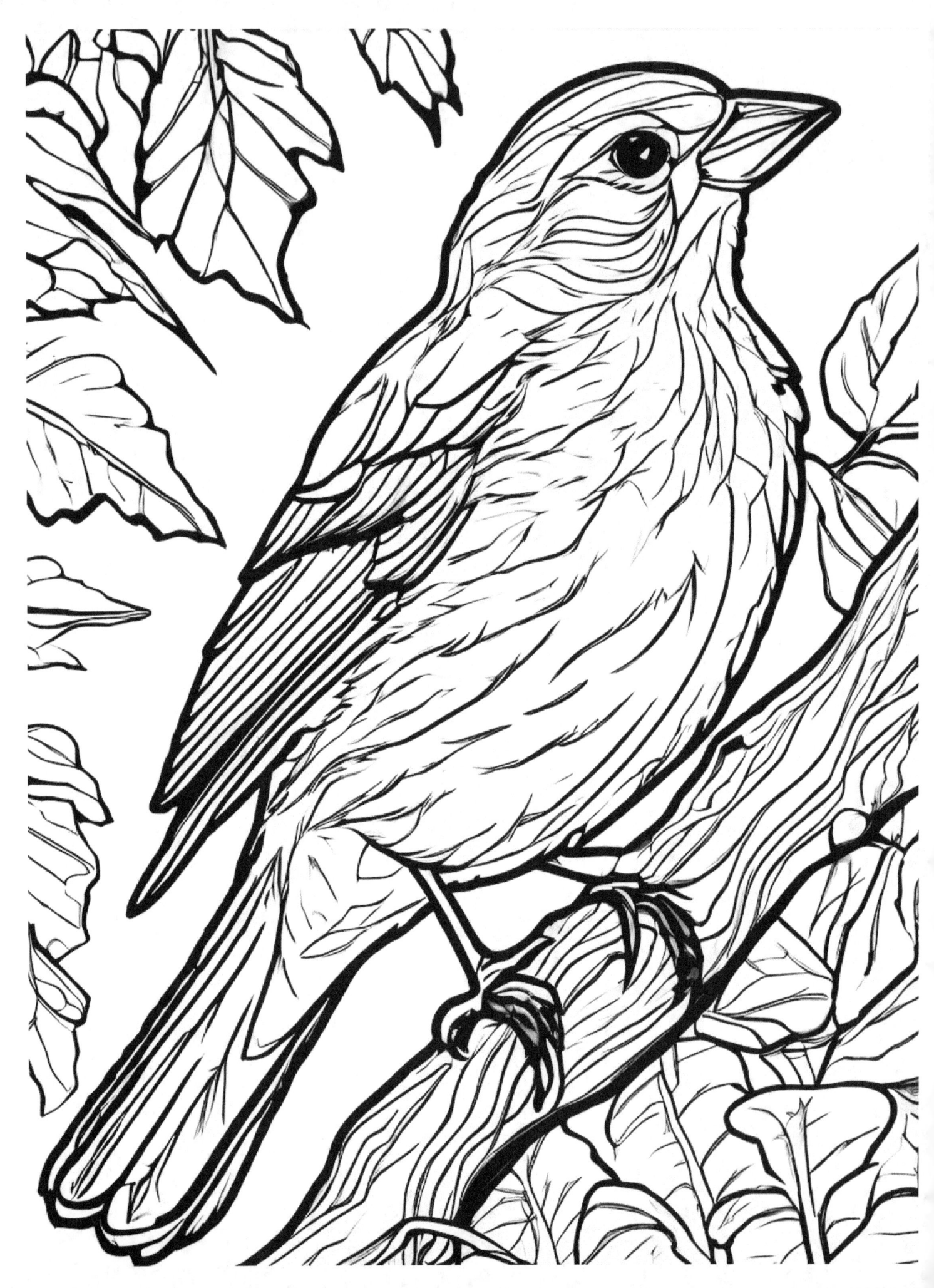

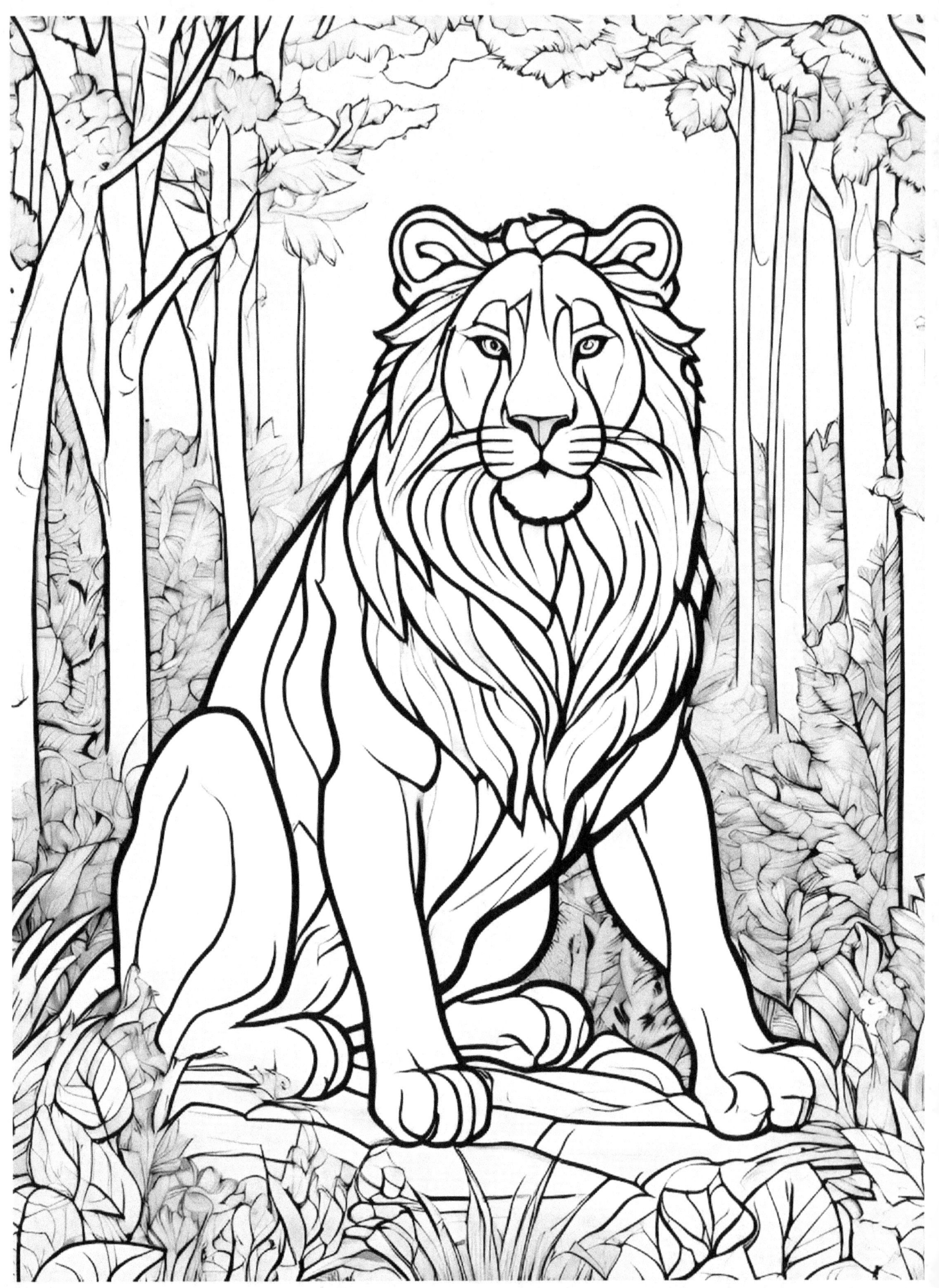

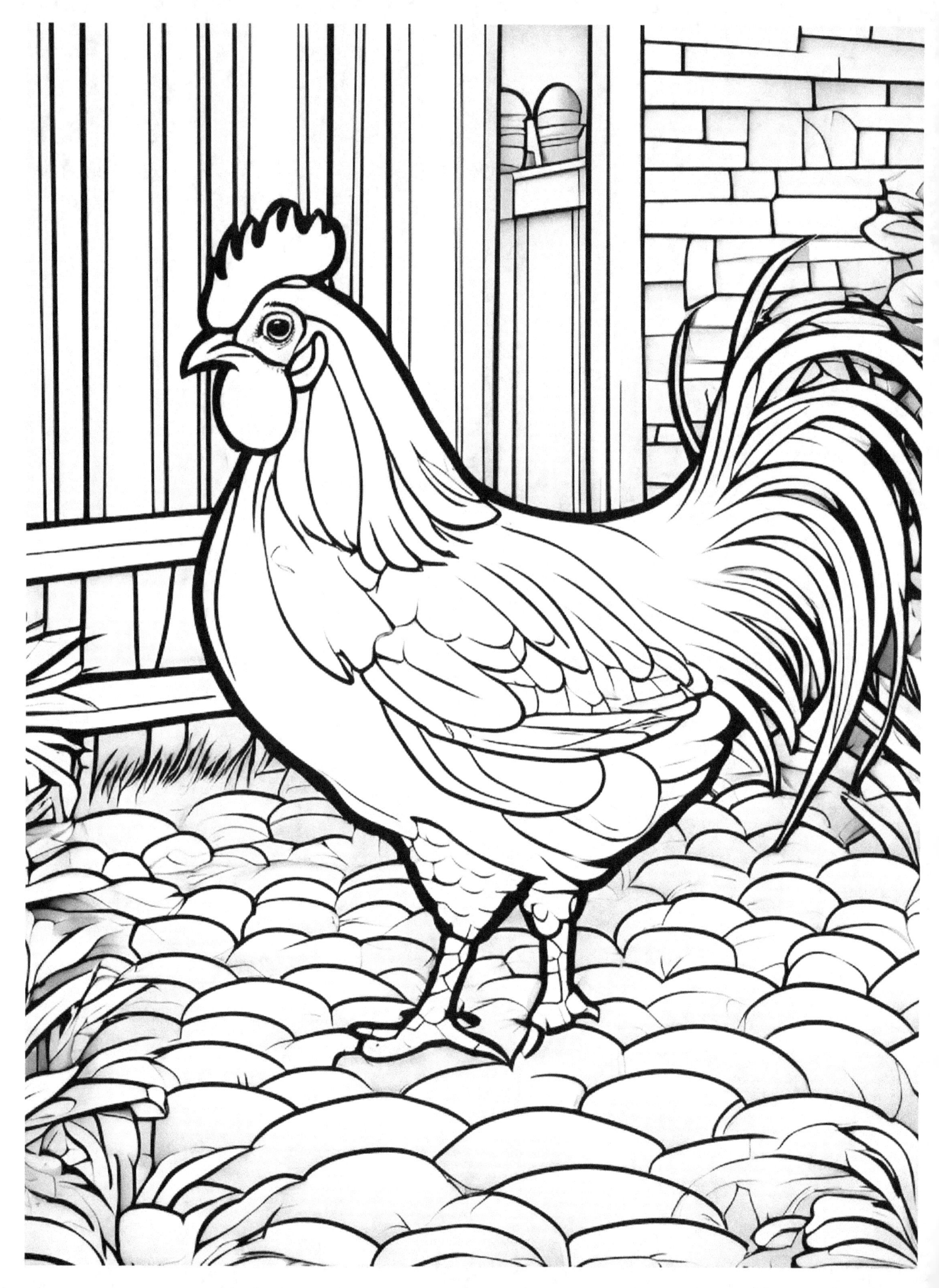

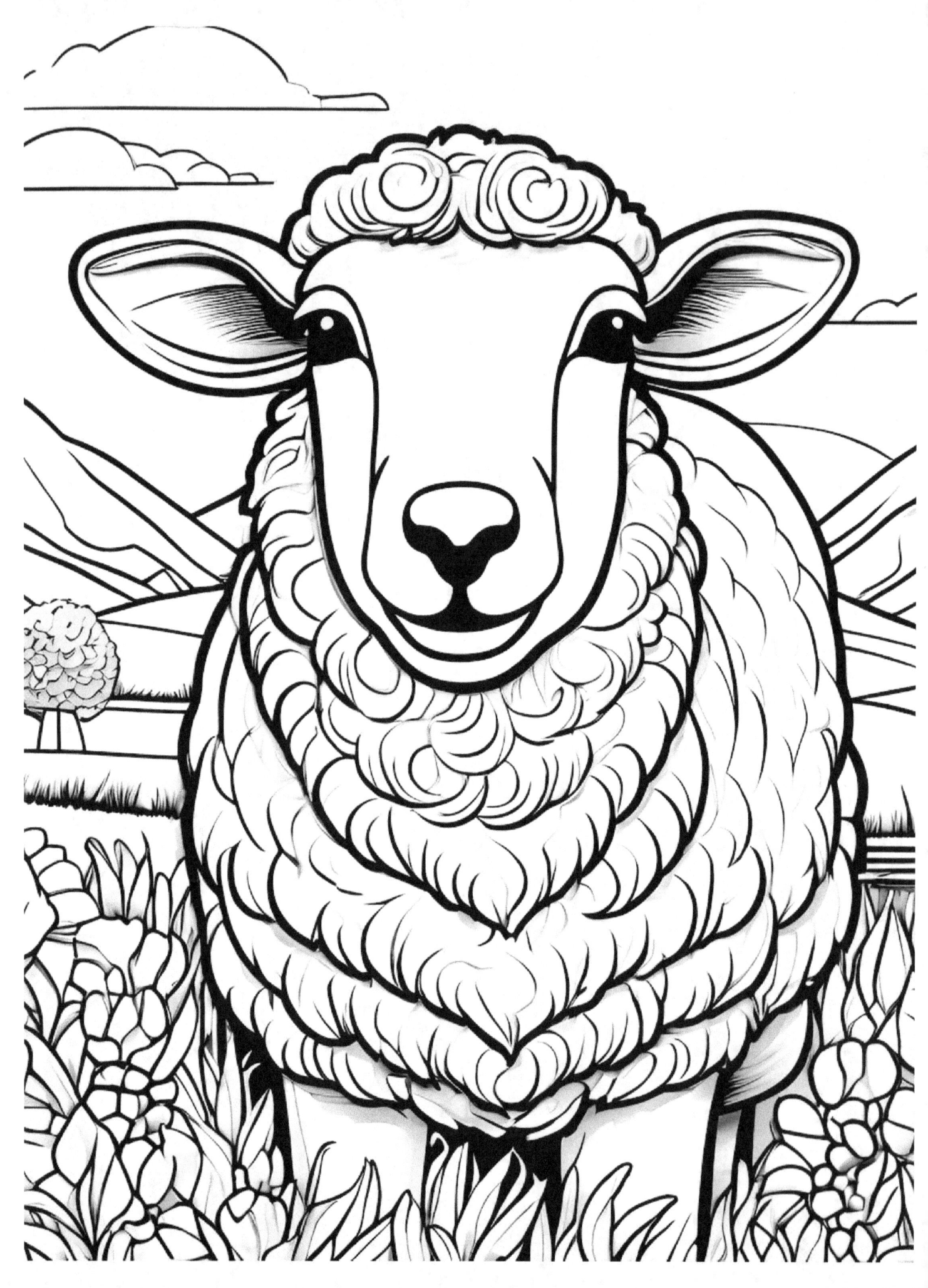

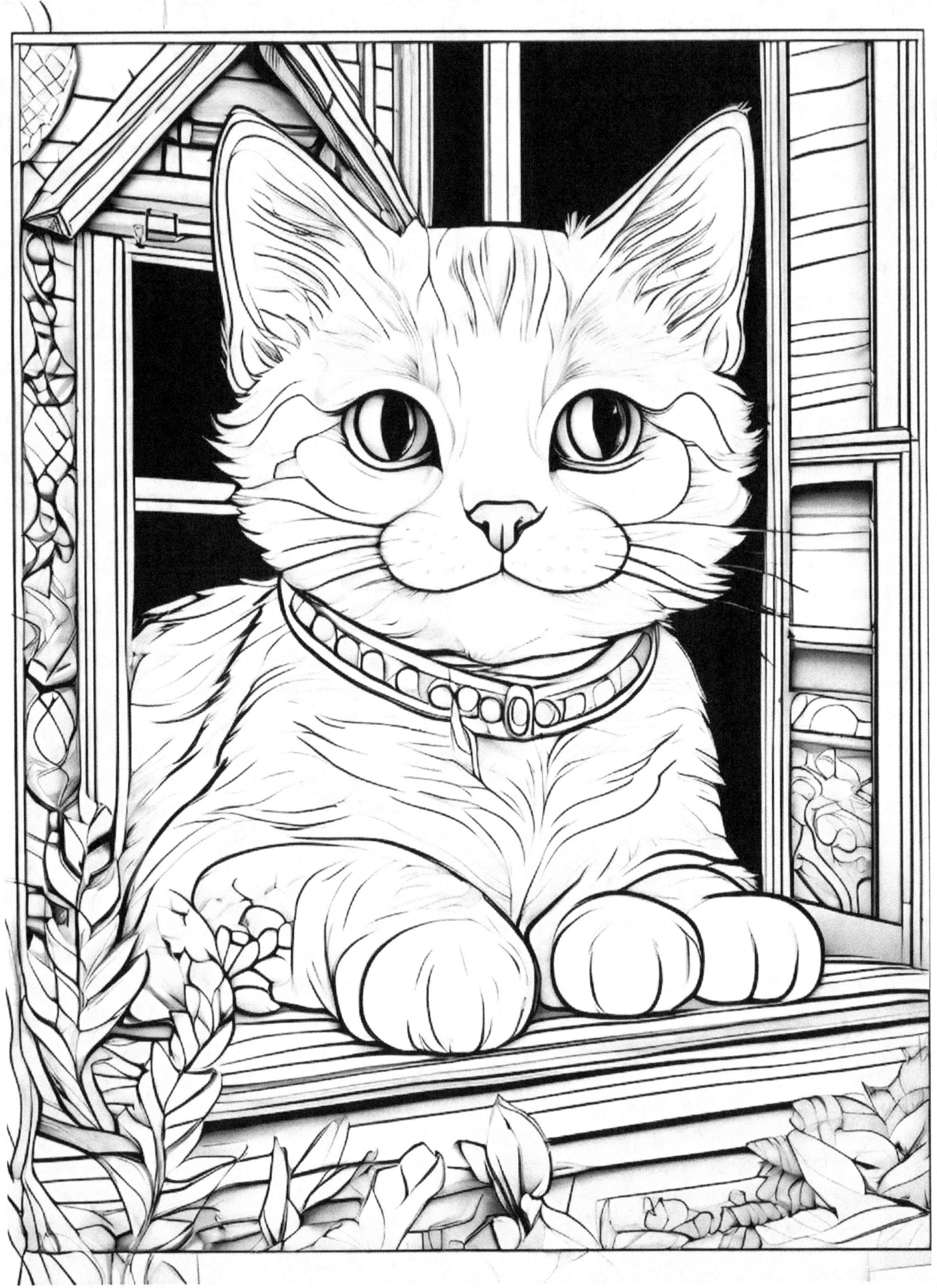

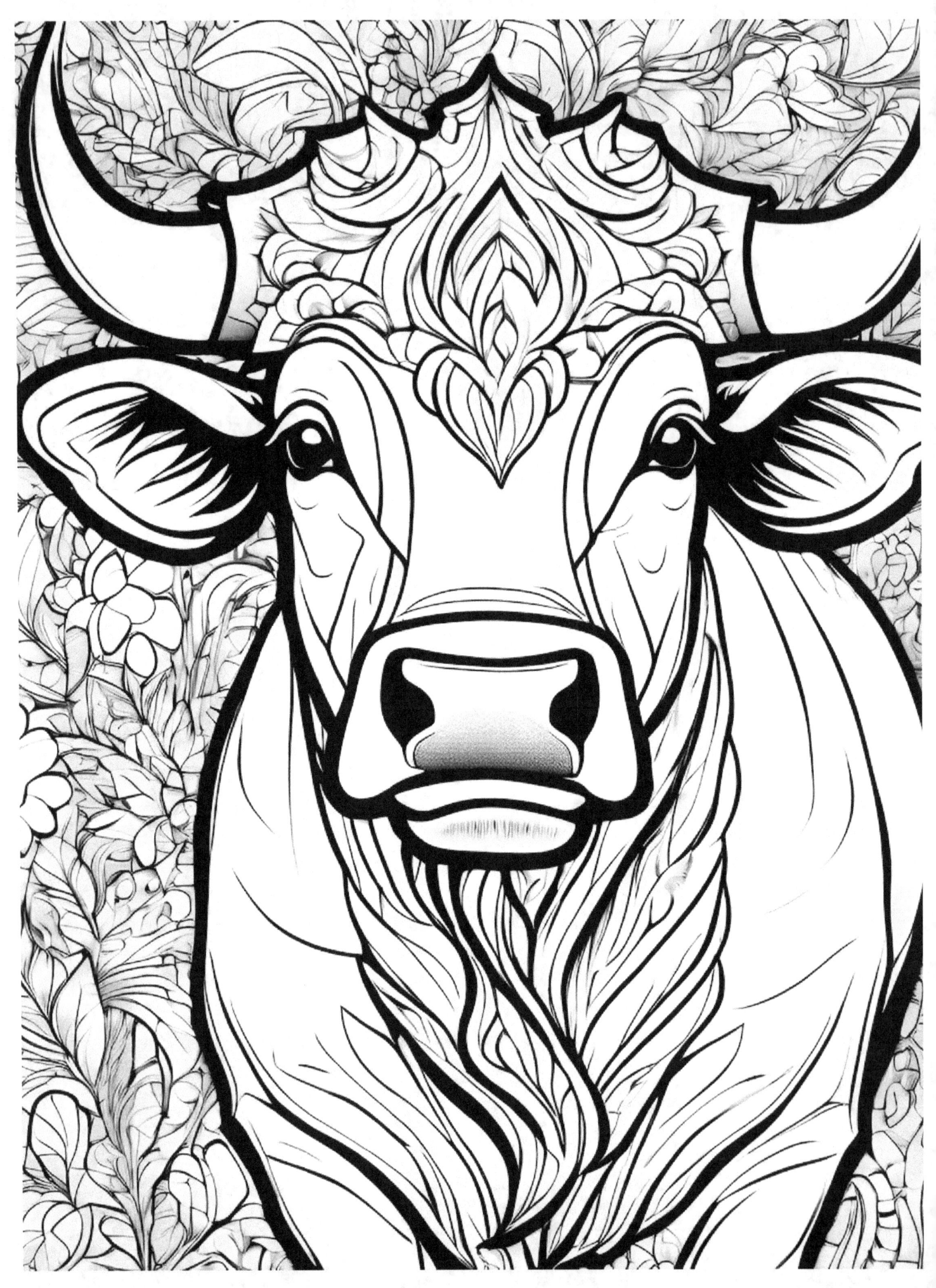

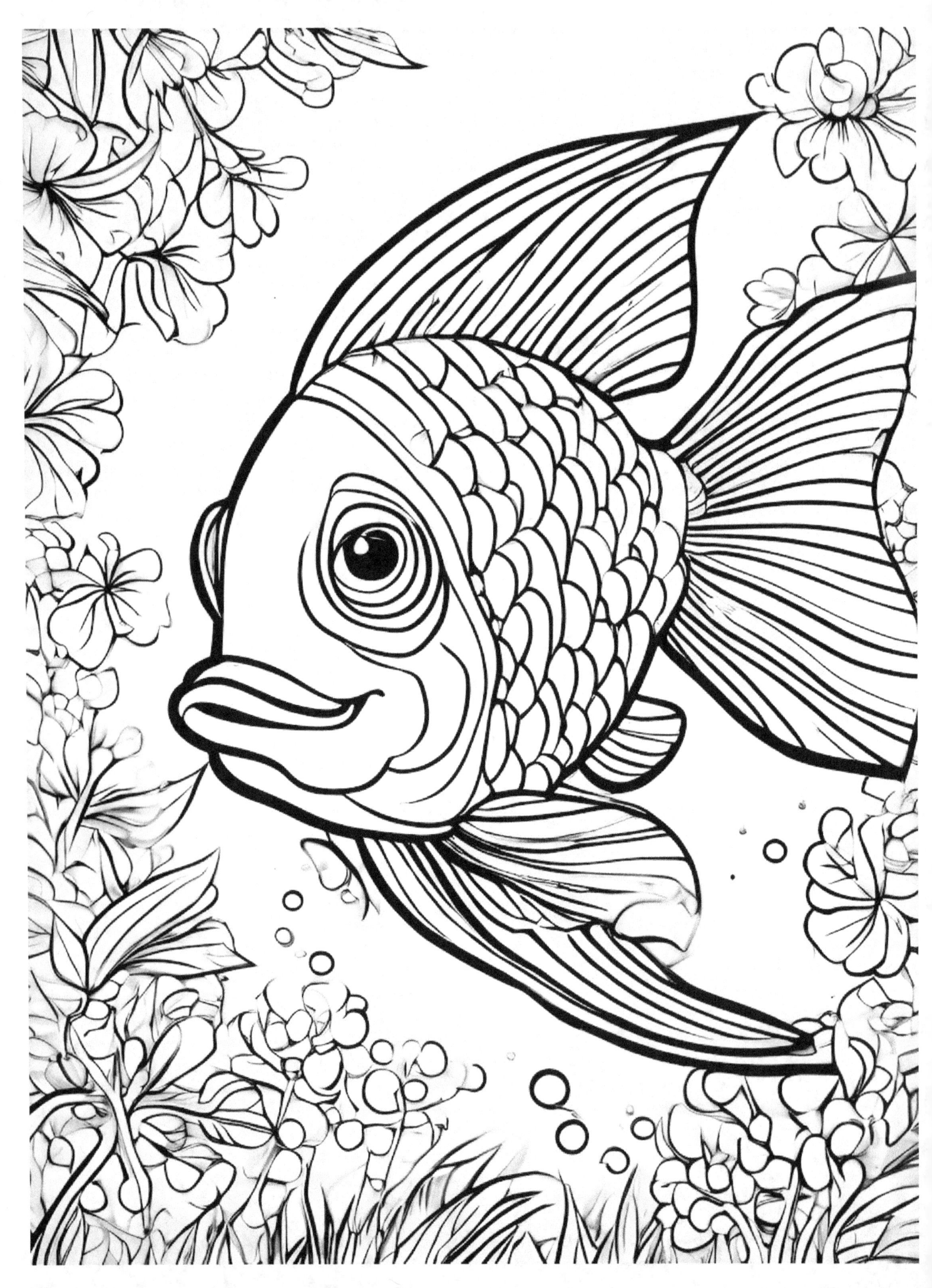

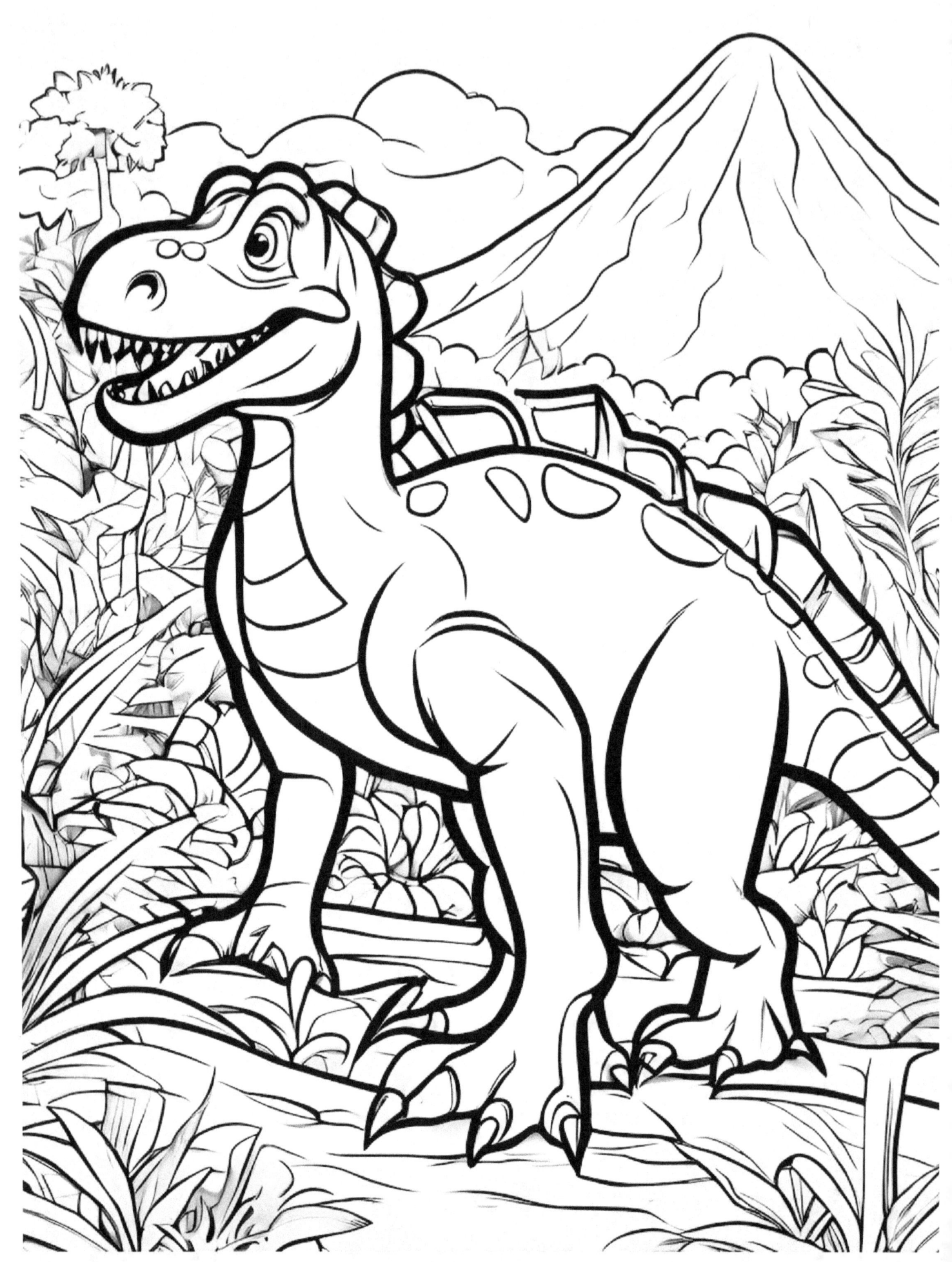

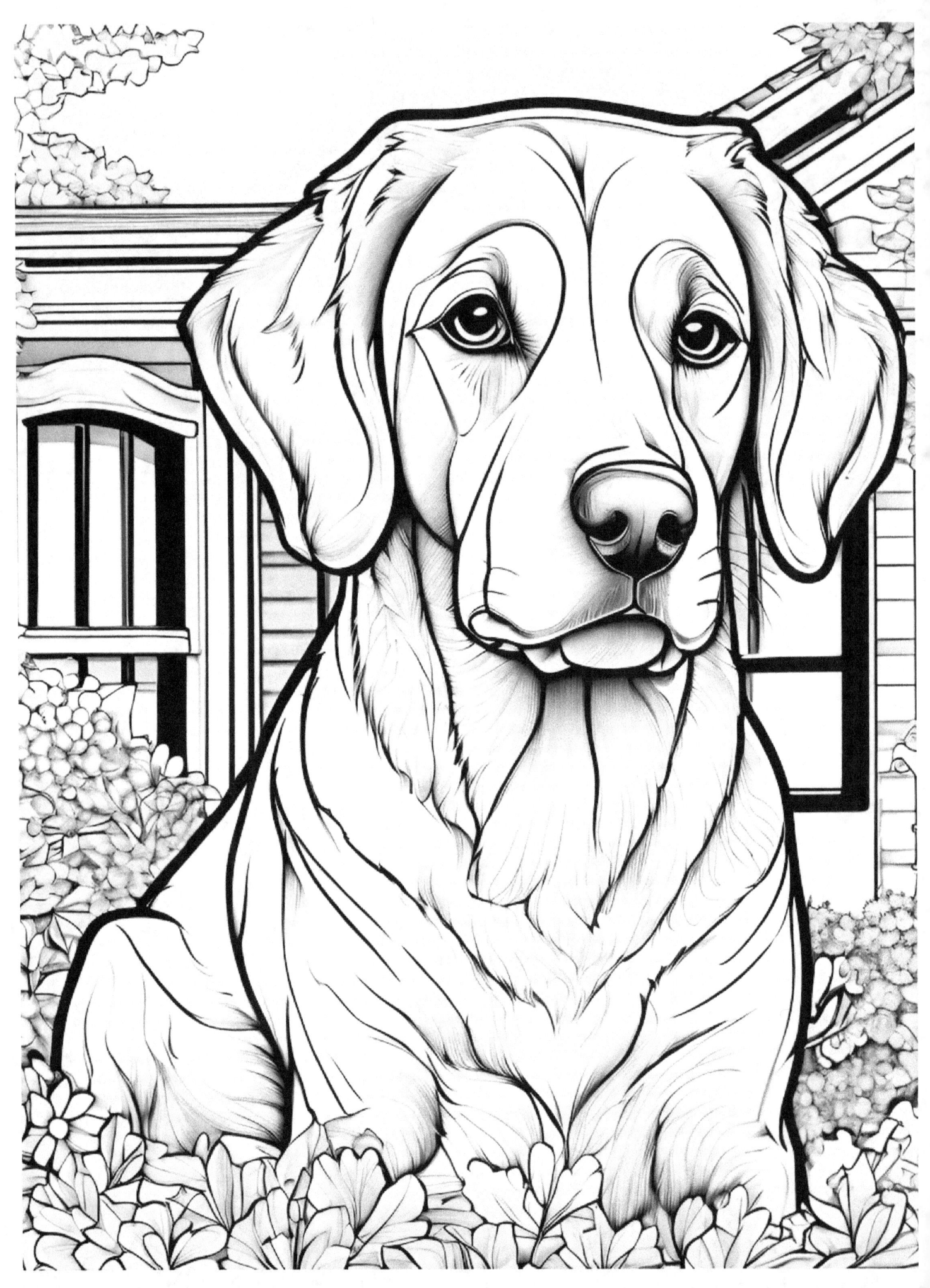